SHAKESPEARE
PROPHET FOR OUR TIME

In this very unusual work, the author, Dr. Henry Douglas Wild, points up the relevance in Shakespeare to the storm of change now enveloping mankind. The prophetic import on our human predicament, he says, can scarcely be exaggerated. The expediency of politics, the futility of war, and the failure of modern man to live by his highest faculties are some of the topics explored in the light of Shakespeare's plays. As Dr. Wild points out, modern youth is especially insistent upon the relevance of learning to the needs of today. In this book we find that Shakespeare speaks clearly to our present generation, reaching across all barriers with a voice that is of life itself. In our complex world of material successes, but glamorized illusions, enslavements, violence and despair, Shakespeare brings to light man's inward path to self-rule and the liberation of his mind. In the final chapter there is a challenge directed particularly to the United States to fulfill its destiny and create a new order for humanity.

Dr. Wild comes from an academic family. He obtained his doctorate at the University of Chicago in 1923, his thesis being "Nature and Democracy in American Literature, from Penn to Whitman." He has had a long career teaching literature, including periods at the University of Minnesota, the University of Michigan, Rutgers University, New Jersey, the University of California in Berkeley, Mills College in Oakland, California, and in adult education. He is now retired and living in California. During his teaching, he never lost enthusiasm for what he considered the main task, stimulating interest in the meaning and value of literature. Shakespeare has always been of particular interest to him, and his love of the Shakespearean plays — his deep comprehension of their message for our time — shine through this book. It is a work that speaks not only to the student of Shakespeare but to all who seek some understanding of and solution to the human crisis.

SHAKESPEARE
PROPHET FOR OUR TIME

HENRY DOUGLAS WILD, Ph.D.

A QUEST BOOK
Published under a grant from The Kern Foundation

THE THEOSOPHICAL PUBLISHING HOUSE
Wheaton, Ill., U.S.A.
Madras, India / London, England

The Theosophical Publishing House, Wheaton, Illinois, is
    a department of The Theosophical Society in America

Original edition 1971
Quest Book edition 1972

ISBN: 0-8356-0421-7

Library of Congress Catalog Number 73-146605

Manufactured in the United States of America

CONTENTS

FOREWORD

In the following discussion we are concerned with Shakespeare's plays as prophetic literature, rooted in ancient wisdom yet pointing forward to a human outlook suited to the needs of the world-wide civilization now in the making. The new phase of existence into which mankind is entering requires for its culture a vision of man capable of effecting the needed subjective transformation. In Shakespeare, despite dated social customs and pageantry, this vision is sufficiently individual yet universal and varied to lead the race toward the needed union of heart and head where the twin laws of freedom and order meet.

The guiding assumption is that the meaning of the plays can be absorbed in a manner capable of yielding what computers cannot; namely, a personal as well as general insight. In its deepest sense this takes the form of a science of self-change through response to what is being enacted. Our adventure will thus consist in exploratory moments of the mystery of being, as these are brought to focus through the symbolic, horizon-like aspect of all experience and made perceivable by poetry.

Shakespeare speaks for the world today. He reaches out to mankind across all barriers with a voice that is of life itself, not an ideology. His timeless revelation is an image of what life can be when man realizes himself as a self-comprehending, self-unified being. In our complex world of material successes, but glamorized illusions, enslavements, violence and despair, Shakespeare brings to light man's inward path to self-rule and the liberation of his mind. He stands at the center of the relevance of all experience. There was never a greater need than now for recognizing the nature of man in the dimensions shown in the Shakespeare plays.

Not only do the plays illustrate the paramount importance of the natural law of balance between freedom and order in human affairs; they also illuminate the growing necessity for man's co-ordination of his inner and his outer life. Like nature herself the plays move as a self-contained and self-revealing force of creative energy, a harmony of opposites like the tide, the rhythmic flow of breathing and the blood stream. The very poetry of the plays serves to dramatize the rhythmic character of the world process by providing the combination of universal meaning and direct appeal. All this is prophetic in a vast, enveloping sense of perspective. It embraces past and future in the nowness of omnipresent life. It gathers up human events into the ongoing cosmic destiny, the "divinity which shapes our ends," whereby, through facing the results of our own thoughts and actions as in a mirror, we learn, as King Lear did, to "see better."

The way Shakespeare is interpreted may be viewed as a cultural index of any age. The following chapters are an attempt to point up relevance in Shakespeare to the storm of change now enveloping mankind. Modern youth is especially insistent upon this relevance of all learning to the far horizon of truth which opens out from life's happenings and renders them fresh and boundless. There is a ground-swell of life-affirmation animating today's youth that has a psychic kinship with the Renaissance spirit which swept over Europe as a regenerating force and permeated the literature of Shakespeare's time.

There is a linkage of relevances between man and the natural world known today as ecology. There is a linkage between concrete fact and the laws of wholeness, freedom, justice, order and beauty which flow out from a realization of Shakespeare's larger meaning. The urgency of this perspective has been increased by the threat to life, human and non-human, posed by the atomic bomb. My prefatory purpose will be served by citing here, as well as in my opening chapter, a statement by Einstein which puts the issue in simple and compelling form. After the horror of Hiroshima, Einstein sent the following telegram to members of the Emergency Committee of Atomic Scientists, of which he was president: "Our world faces a crisis as yet unperceived by those possessing the power to make great decisions. . . . The unleashed power of the atom has changed everything save our ways of thinking, and thus we drift to an unparalleled catastrophe. A new way of thinking is essential if man is to survive and move toward higher levels."*

In these prophetic words the vision of the great scientist and that of Shakespeare join, uniting science, art, philosophy and ethics at the highest level of thought in dedication to the human struggle for peace. Tragedy had already overtaken the world when Einstein's energy formula, $E = MC^2$, was seized for the construction of the atomic bomb.

The answer to this issue lies in the hearts of men undivided by the separative mind. For this reason it places the relevance of Shakespearean drama, together with the humanitarian purpose of Einstein, in a perspective of unsurpassed importance for our time. In the spotlight of this issue of life and death the psychic totality and creative dynamics of the plays must needs be brought to bear on the deep and inward processes of human knowing.

An obstacle to grasping this import for our times lies in the customary approach to the plays as separate units, and the lack of study in depth when they are presented to the student in schools generally. Thus their meaning as the total unitary vision and life-flow of one man, the poet himself, is neglected. This totality of vision is a priceless truth in itself. It consists in the mystery of life becoming knowable as a potential wholeness of being in all men. It is the stretching of mind and heart toward comprehensiveness, the self-knowing of man as the measure of all things. Man needs today, as a balancing factor, the liberating awareness of consciousness, the life-principle within himself. It is only by going within that he may find the "new way of thinking" he desperately needs, the axis of identity which unites him with all existence.

What is new in the present discussion is the attempt, particularly in the final chapter, to bring this wisdom to bear on life in these United States. A new type of American youth is seeking beyond the mind for a more total vision than modern education is providing. It is for this new youth

---

* Antonina Vallentin: *The Drama of Albert Einstein.*

that the present study is primarily intended.

Also in the final chapter appear suggested linkages between Shakespeare's and Einstein's vision of man and the meaning of the motto on the Reverse Seal of the United States: Novus Ordo Seclorum, A New Order of the Ages. Today's hurricane of change may rightly be regarded as the birthpangs of a new order, a "new way of thinking" for the new age.

In a world technologically conquerable by force but lacking man's understanding of the law of cosmic-human entirety (another term for his identity with life), our modern claim to educate the whole man is a mockery. The relevance of this issue appears sharply in our interpretation of Hamlet's matchless soliloquy on man. Shakespeare put into the mouth of Hamlet the magnitude of self-ignorance which separates man from his noble possibilities. It is ironic that the vast reach of Hamlet's eloquence and meaning is traditionally passed off as a flight of poetry or a bit of play-acting. On the surface it is an account of his depression over the state of affairs at court and the burden of his pretended madness. This is only the foreground of his feeling of tragedy; the main reason for this feeling is his generalized conclusion as to the condition of man, in consequence of which the earth itself loses its meaning, and the very firmament appears to be only "a foul and pestilent congregation of vapours."

The poet's expression of the essential dignity of man is strikingly expressed in the lines:

> What a piece of work is a man! How noble in reason! How infinite in faculty, in form and moving! How express and admirable in action! How like an angel in apprehension! How like a god! The beauty of the world!
>
> Hamlet, Act II, Sc. ii, lines 315-319

The positive-negative terms of this issue reach their climactic summation when those words of Hamlet are succeeded by his expression of weariness and disgust with the world's condition and the treachery and violence of the situation around him. The Shakespearean issue for our time

is in the similar contrast between man's godlike potentiali-
ties as "the beauty of the world" and his present-day destructiveness. The prophetic import on our human predicament
can scarcely be exaggerated. Actually, however, the intended
meaning extends to the whole of man's scheme of knowledge, including our modern crisis. Objective knowledge
must be linked to self-knowledge if we would avoid distorting our adjustment to the scheme of existence. The poet's
intent is to reach out beyond Hamlet's personal fate in order
to deliver a warning against disasters arising from man's
ignorance of himself.

Shakespeare's use of drama in *Hamlet* must thus be viewed
in correlation with Einstein's appeal for "a new way of
thinking." Together these prophetic implications point the
direction toward which our human cultural system must be
oriented. It is simple realism to hold that man's happiness
as well as his security lies in his living in harmonic unity
with the world.

Here we come close to Bacon's warning in his *Novum
Organum* regarding man's failure to interpret fully and cor-
rectly nature's laws of analogy. "The correspondence between the architectures and fabrics of things natural and
things civil" must not be regarded as merely "similitudes or
fancies, but plainly the same footsteps of nature treading
and printing upon different subjects."

Here the issue in human affairs is the recognition of a
universal law of identity linking the works of man to the
cosmos. In the symbolism of the plays we are offered affirmation of the reality of these laws.

Consider in this perspective the profound meaning contained in the lines spoken by Isabel in *Measure for Measure,*
a passage unmatched in literature for depth and brevity:

> but man, proud man,
> Dressed in a little brief authority,
> Most ignorant of what he's most assur'd,
> His glassy essence, like an angry ape
> Plays such fantastic tricks before high heaven
> As make the angels weep.
>
> Act II, Sc. ii, lines 117-122

By implication and inference throughout the plays the practical meaning of "glassy essence" appears repeatedly as the key to our total human adjustment to existence. It applies pointedly to Romeo's instinctive resolve in the midst of life's warring human opposites: "Turn back, dull earth, and find thy center out." (*Romeo and Juliet*, Act II, Sc. ii, line 2) Man is to discover and apply his own central intelligence to achieve liberating self-knowledge in whatever particular race, creed, sex, nationality, family or work he finds himself.

In the term "glassy essence" Shakespeare is transcending the limits of conceptual language. He is referring to the absolute reality and living fact of the indivisibility of life's infinitude out of which everything comes. This is not an abstraction, but is a "presence," the non-particular which is in all particulars, the non-thought which is in all thought. It constitutes the selfhood of all that is. Man's path to the heart of life's mystery is through his own heart, opened to the silent spaces of consciousness. The deathless mission of the plays is to open and explore these spaces.

Chapter I

THE RELEVANCE OF SHAKESPEARE TODAY

> Thank God the time is now when wrong
> Comes up to face us everywhere,
> Never to leave us 'til we take
> The longest stride of soul men ever took.
> Affairs are now soul size.
> The enterprise
> Is exploration unto God.
> *A Sleep of Prisoners,* Christopher Fry

These lines state the case of our human situation in this twentieth century. They define our dilemma and our opportunity by linking them together. They place man in his rightful position between them, where the challenge of disaster opens the door on horizons of assurance that adequate means of salvaging our modern world by spiritualizing it are at hand if only we will comprehend and use them.

The present approach to the Shakespeare plays is undertaken in the belief, long ripening into conviction, that they constitute a world bridge of practical wisdom and beauty spanning the chasm of confusion which has opened so dangerously across this century's line of advance toward a new, more integrative civilization.

Our Crisis in Consciousness

For centuries our human order has been building up a titanic confrontation of man with himself, an encounter solvable only by a radical revolution in his own mind. The

issue is not "compete or perish," but an ability to "see better." Such was Kent's seed of wisdom, planted in Lear's
mind at the moment of the latter's fateful misjudgment, to
bear fruit only after a tempest of agony.

Both the *Lear* story and the *Book of Job* frequently have
been pondered as dramas of man's ordeal of self-facing and
transformation. Nevertheless, our state of dividedness has
reached the point of an impending intercultural explosion.
It is this fact which calls for our examining the holistic nature of reality in the Shakespeare plays. Since the suffering
of man today arises from a complex partitioning of his understanding of himself and his motives, we are obligated
to draw upon the world's major resources of wisdom in their
least controversial, most appealing and applicable form.

We are now in a crucial phase of a crisis in consciousness, and our need, like Lear's, is for a more total awareness
and testing of all experience. This means a direct inward
facing of what we are and are not. The current temptation
to demand "law and order" — the outer form — while denying the inner law of justice, is but one of the typical areas
of our modern confusion which Shakespeare illuminates.

Today the fate of nations and the whole issue of war and
peace are in the hands of men equipped with unparalleled
destructive power, yet who lack adequate knowledge of
who or what man is and how he may be able to surmount
meaninglessness and violence. Men need the sense of direction and the courage of the whole man to follow it by
taking adequate initiatives for peace.

The relevance of the plays to our world problems lies in
the fact that they are mirrorings of life itself, containing
keys to what is universally human in man, regardless of the
state of culture or the age in which he lives. Their appeal
to the Zulus of Africa is proof that despite the difference
in social conditions, people everywhere have a living desire
for the spirit of essential man which they find in the plays.

Conversely, a decline in vision such as afflicts the over-
sophisticated civilization now appearing in the world is
marked by a falling off of recognition of the wisdom which
speaks from behind the ethical structure of the plays. The
irony of this situation is that Shakespeare oriented his pro-

ductions to the very quality of understanding which has been neglected in their study. The "soul size" aspect of the issue cannot be grasped by a rationalization which excludes the necessary attitude of receptivity toward life. Man cannot perceive his true identity by separating his consciousness from a total awareness, outside and within.

From these observations it is clear that the present discussion is a departure from the traditional view of the Shakespeare plays as "literature." Instead it seeks to provide evidence that what the great author intended above all was to bestow upon mankind an imaginative means of "exploration unto God." As to this, the plays still belong to the future; yet it is a future that is present in all its force and meaning now.

Our civilization today points to the absolute need of a directive vision for the wise use of the energies of nature. Our cultural lag in this respect demands that the reflective principle within us be awakened by the most consummate means available. Taken in their entirety, the plays serve this purpose incomparably, mirroring as they do the interplay of all human powers in the light of a destiny which unites in one Reality the personal and the universal levels of our being. Modern man's search for meaning, if carried far enough, will lead him to the intangibles behind the facts in the plays. This inmost experience is a form of yoga.

Along these lines the groundwork of psychological investigation laid down by Jung opens fresh approaches to the plays. This psychology has a strong affinity with the ancient wisdom which Shakespeare had absorbed. Jung's conception of the unconscious appearing in myth, metaphor and symbol as "the other side of consciousness" will be viewed in the dramatic structures to be examined as an integrative and vitalizing potential in man's response to his experiences in life.

Never before has the plight of the world required of each human being such an all-out giving of himself to the Promethean adventure of self-knowledge, self-testing and perfecting. For four centuries western man has been looking into the Shakespearean scene as into a mirror for taking the measure of himself. Yet because he has failed to look with sufficient wholeness of perception, the image he has caught and pondered has been fragmentary.

If man is to have peace in his world, he must find in himself this key to the balance of freedom and order. It means a rhythmic harmony of the centripetal and centrifugal energies of his own consciousness, a union seldom achieved, but one which is the poetry of the plays and of all human existence.

The four-hundredth Shakespearean anniversary has come and gone. But in the outpouring of world-wide acclaim and fresh appraisal there has been all but total silence on the realm of being from which the plays draw their rounded vision of life. Without recognition of the invisible dimensions of man's social or historical experience as depicted in the plays, their prophetic function in helping to interpret our age of change within a frame of timeless reality is obscured if not obliterated.

Unfortunately our need of a more total vision of ourselves and our ways is not recognized by the world at large, as evidenced by the following quotations from widely different sources:

> Mankind must put an end to war, or war will put an end to mankind. (John F. Kennedy)

> Since the splitting of the atom everything has changed save our ways of thinking, and thus we drift towards an unparalleled catastrophe. (Albert Einstein)

> The world is now too dangerous for anything but the truth; it is now too small for anything but brotherhood. (Rev. A. Powell Davies)

> Things fall apart; the center cannot hold: Mere anarchy is loosed upon the world . . . The best lack all conviction, while the worst are full of passionate intensity. (William Butler Yeats)

> What we dare not face is not total extinction, but total meaninglessness. (David Riesman)

The correlations to be found between these current matters and many of the Shakespeare themes are direct and explicit, despite differences in time, place and circumstance.

This imaginative bridging of time gaps is significant for several reasons. Among them is the capacity it develops for gazing past our experiences as through an arch into an untraveled world of larger horizons whither the race is moving toward liberation from its "Midsummer Night's Dream" of animality, self-dividedness, violence and war.

In a fundamental sense the case made by Paul Tillich for the need to recover the lost dimension of depth in religion applies equally to the plays. In both instances remedial action begins with what Tillich terms "a radical realization of our predicament."

The present venture is an attempt to show how intellectualized instruction may be subordinated to a free creative absorption of the wisdom the plays bring to light as a visible flowering of the interior life of man. The view here proposed is that the plays constitute mankind's most comprehensive laboratory in motivation research — not for exploiting our fellow men, but for universalizing ourselves in a divided world.

New studies, such as that of the Oedipus complex in Hamlet's relation to his mother, mark a psychoanalytical trend. Nevertheless, such investigations are pursued along lines which lead away from, rather than toward, the large psychosynthesis the plays require for a rightly proportioned understanding. The desire to prove a case within the context of Freudian categories and procedures inevitably runs the risk of grave distortions. This is likely to arise from a misplaced centering of focus.

The thesis underlying the present study is that the plays exist for one supreme purpose: the awakening of human souls to their spiritual nature and destiny. The central dramatic theme to which everything else is subsidiary is held to be the gradual transition from man's sense of identity with the "angry ape" in him to an awareness of his godlike "glassy essence." These terms, used by Isabel in *Measure for Measure*, (Act II, Sc. ii, line 120) fix the poles between which the characters in all thirty-six plays live out the self-chosen patterns of their lives. They correspond closely to the biblical distinction between the "dead" and the "quick".

To clarify and expedite this study, we cite the summation

of human wisdom known in theosophical literature as "The Three truths":*

> The soul of man is immortal, and its future is the future of a thing whose growth and splendor have no limit.
> The principle which gives life dwells in us and without us, is undying and eternally beneficent, is not heard or seen or felt, but is perceived by the man who desires perception.
> Each man is his own absolute law-giver, the dispenser of glory or gloom to himself; the decree-er of his life, his reward, his punishment.

These guidelines for entering the world of essential man in Shakespeare necessitate first a "radical realization" of the predicament we bring upon ourselves by our highly sophisticated ignorance of our own ignorance. Matched against our mechanistic definitions of our problems, the Three Truths oblige us to test everything anew. They challenge us to consider what we do to ourselves by our own acts, and to stop dehumanizing ourselves by becoming machine-like. They focus the responsibility we bear for our technologically acquisitive society and its upset of the balance of nature and man alike.

As we seek to apply these "Truths," we discover finally that the law of proportion which they express is the inner face of justice.

The primacy of this central principle is negated by our tendency to view politics, jurisprudence, even law itself, as material force. Judgments based on value are likely to be subordinated or denied as subjective opinions only, whereas power is a fact, its expression is an observable event, and pious wishes as to what ought to be have no scientific validity.

It has been truly said that we are caught between extremes of blind faith and materialistic skepticism and that only the ancient wisdom can stop it. Hence it is time for theosophy to enter the arena, including the study of Shakespeare.

---

* *The Idyll of the White Lotus* by Mabel Collins. The Theosophical Publishing House, Madras, India

Finding Center or Identity

Wherever there is action there is change, and change implies a pivotal center around which it takes place within a surrounding field of wholeness. In human life, as in physics, the process of change is to be understood in relation to some law or principle which is changeless and therefore serves as a base or point of reference and leverage for our understanding. The analogy of the pole star as a guide to travelers is an example.

In a parallel way the extent of man's fear of change is an exact index of his lack of knowledge of who or where he is. At present his anxiety is doubled by the fact that the speed of the changes occurring in the world is matched by his loss of grip on a center of reality or meaning within himself. His plight therefore consists in the urgency of his need to find that center which can "hold."

This holding is possible only when the center is determined by a sense of identity with the wholeness of life itself. Without the healing atmosphere of proportion and well-being which wholeness confers upon our living, we fail to find our integral place in the scheme of things. The finding of identity by an awareness distinct from emotional or mental assumption is what the plays are intended to induce by means of example.

Thus in this preliminary way we have arrived at the turning point of our human crisis and likewise a still largely unexplored frontier in the Shakespeare plays. Humanity is facing a change of direction in the course of its evolution where the choice of identity between the material self and the spiritual self is at decisive issue. It is in this context, therefore, that the borderline in man between the "angry ape" and the "glassy essence," has to be explored. The entire remainder of this discussion will hinge upon it. The implementing of the plays to this end is among the foremost cultural needs of the time.

For illustration of the drift of these remarks let us turn to the crisis of identity or true self-knowledge, on which all of the plays swing, as revealed in the third act of *Julius Caesar*. As the conspirators gather at the Capitol before the assassination, Caesar, to avoid giving an impression of weakness, refuses to revoke the banishment of a conspirator's brother. In the same spirit of political fear of seeming to be afraid, he had rejected the warnings of a soothsayer and of his own wife as to the risk of going to the Capitol on the Ides of March. In boastful language he declares, "But I am as constant as the northern star" (Act III, Sc. i, line 60) ; in three more minutes he is dead.

It may be conceded that in Caesar's thought of himself he was unshakeable in his dedication to the Roman national cause. However, if we regard his likening of himself to the northern star as an authentic case of a higher order of experience or identity, we are at odds with the typical Shakespearean handling of such matters. This is true on two counts.

First, the plays abound in instances of great oaths made by characters in personal difficulty, particularly when they are defying deep ethical or spiritual principles. Invariably these self-assumed invocations of the power of status by means of cosmic or mythological images recoil upon and confound the utterer.

Second, Caesar meant this self-image of constancy to be taken at face value, whereas this ran counter to what he must have surmised was an inner law, as indicated by the combined testimony of the soothsayer and his wife's dream. In such a conflict the Shakespearean view consistently supports the side of esoteric validity, and modern psychologists emphasize that man disregards this hidden angle of reality at his peril.

In justice to Caesar's actual greatness and historic impact, however, we should note that following his assassination the rest of the play strikingly reveals the post-mortem influence of this statesmanship as a continuing force in human affairs.

For another example, we have in *Richard II* the spectacle of a weak king vainly endeavoring to identify with the king image he had made of himself. The crises he had brought upon the kingdom began when, in the name of peace, he called off a duel between Henry Bolingbroke and the Duke of Norfolk over the murder of the Duke of Gloucester, an affair in which Richard was not innocent. His act of banishing the two contending dukes under the guise of mercy was one of fear as well as hypocrisy, and when Henry returned to England a few years later with an army, Richard was fatally in trouble.

After learning that Welsh forces supporting him had disbanded, the king is told by his friend, the Duke of Aumerle, that he is looking pale and is reminded, "Remember who you are."

At this reference to his identity Richard confesses:

> I had forgot myself; am I not king?
> Awake, thou sluggard majesty! Thou sleepest.
> > Act III, Sc. ii, lines 83-84

In the next act Richard is curious to learn how his feeling of identity shows in his face and calls for a mirror. On contrasting what he sees with the pomp and glory he remembers, he dashes the glass to the ground and in this gesture unconsciously prefigures the deposing and death he was to bring upon himself.

We see in this play an instance of the author's use of history for revealing a particular cause of national disaster; namely, the existence of vanity, egoism, a false royalty or sense of identity at the highest level of authority. Richard had his gifts and qualities, but material selfhood was the deciding factor and resulted in a century of feuding which led to the War of the Roses.

In *Othello* we have the tragedy of man as "angry ape," devoid of any glimmering of his spiritual nature. The career of Iago in deliberately pursuing a course of psychological crime reaches a pitch of almost unbearable intensity in its consequences.

The play has hardly more than begun when Iago casually reveals the key to his character as he confides to Roderigo, "I am not what I am." (Act I, Sc. i, line 65). We fail to catch the terrible import of this statement until the closing scenes of the play, but by then we are likely to be too shaken to think back and see in those simple words the horror of an absolute negation.

Not only in Iago but behind Othello's twofold act in destroying Desdemona and then himself lies the core of the

problem of identity. In the first of the Othello instances it
is the torture of the hero's conflict between love, or symbolically, the light of his own soul typified by Desdemona,
and the alienation of his mind from her, caused by his fear-
ful clinging to false evidence or mere appearance as distinct
from reality. In the second case it is Othello's desperate effort to rid himself of the evil which is the cause of his suffering by taking his own life, at the same time seeking to
slay his remembered enemy, the Turk, now associated with
Iago as a living presence in his own breast.

The entire tragedy is that of man's failure to heed the
voice of intuition and look beyond the limits which the
separated mind imposes on existence. The individual and
social implications of *Othello* from the standpoint of man's
self-responsibility are limitless. If, as *Light on the Path**
points out, man is unable to perceive the light of wisdom
in his own heart, it is useless for him to look for it else-
where. Thus the more powerful or destructive he becomes,
the more colossal is his error. This applies to nations as
well as to individuals.

To bring this central issue of identity into the sharpest
contrast, try placing together "honest" Iago's "I am not
what I am" and God's divine affirmation to Moses, "I am
That I am." No more compelling revelation of the central
meaning in human destiny is conceivable.

In our universe of contrasts thus brought to ultimate focus
in man, what, then, are these opposites of selfhood? What,
for instance, is Iago's own awareness of what he is? We may
describe him as a type so inwardly unrelated to other beings
that life is but a game of manipulation for him to take advantage of. He is pure isolated intellect, a condition Emerson described as "the devil." As such he becomes the calcu-
lating "slayer of the Real."

The divine affirmation, on the contrary, from the eternal
and omnipresent Source, is Self-knowledge, pure "glassy
essence." It is a shadowless indestructible light perceiving
its own infinitude.

In terms of consciousness, illusion is the shadow the mind

---

* *Light on the Path* by Mabel Collins, The Theosophical Publishing
House, Wheaton, Illinois.

projects across the field of intuitive perception, whereas the light of intuition galvanized by the pure essence of mind freed of its dross, is capable of lifting man out of his self-shadow. The point of immediate bearing is the fact that throughout the Shakespeare plays this "discipline of the Ancients" may be seen and felt as an influence spurring man to blend his mind and soul.

In its extreme form, so evident these days, the paralyzing despair and gloom of the "shadow," or sense of meaningless-ness in life, found poignant expression in the nihilistic fa-talism of Poe's *The Raven*. Light from the lamp over the doorway is intercepted by the raven perched on the bust of Pallas, and the poet sinks into identification with the shadow instead of with the light:

> And my soul from out the shadow that lies
> floating on the floor
> Shall be lifted — nevermore.

There is much pathos and need for compassionate under-standing in the case of Poe's personal plight. Similarly in these days of intellectualized blurring of the true poetic function it is important to realize the need of those mag-netic threads of correlation between head and heart and be-tween man and nature which are woven into the Shake-speare plays. This is indicated figuratively by two of the well-known lines in *A Midsummer Night's Dream*:

> The poet's eye in a fine frenzy rolling,
> Doth glance from heaven to earth, from earth to hea-
> ven . . .
>
> Act V, Sc. i, lines 13-14

In ancient Greece, as Werner Jaeger points out, the dy-namics of creative inspiration were expressed by the term *psychogogia*, signifying soul-training. It referred to art's power of transcending both the intellect and the senses by combining universal significance with concrete appeal. In other words, it is a blending of intuition and the concrete mind, a uniting of heaven and earth.

Our present discussion of these psychic matters reverts, however, to the tragic implications of *Othello* for the crisis in man today. The whole issue of human welfare, even survival, hangs on the Iago problem of identity: the question of who is man? When one of our contemporary statesmen ended an important address with this question, he was leaving the decision between peace and the likelihood of a worldwide holocaust up to the limited self-knowledge and untrained vision of people everywhere.

At bottom it is the Mephistophelian struggle of the material intellect for complete ascendancy over heart and conscience. The weapon used is the denial of spiritual selfhood.

Prophetically considered, *Othello* is a most powerful commentary on the crisis of twentieth century man's imbalance, brought on by an exclusively physical identification of himself. A further bearing of the play on our time, that of the harm done by the deliberate sowing of the seeds of suspicion, fear and hate, will be reserved for later discussion.

Another drama of identity, *Romeo and Juliet,* although tragic, will help to offset this scheme of darkness with its imperishable light.

The play opens with an extraordinary structuring of dualities. A very distinct pairing both of characters and incidents runs through the framework built up in the first act, beginning with the first lines. This sets the psychological stage for all that follows.

The quarreling between the servingmen of the feuding houses of Capulet and Montague leads swiftly to a clash of arms, intensified as Benvolio and Tybalt come on the scene, this to be followed by the entrance of old Capulet and Montague with their respective wives.

When Romeo appears, we have his first reaction to the fray, stated in terms of a psychological dilemma:

> Here's much to do with hate, but more with love.
> Why, then, O brawling love! O loving hate!
> O anything of nothing first create!
> O heavy lightness! Serious vanity!
> Mis-shapen Chaos of well-seeming forms!
> > Act I, Sc. i, lines 181-185

This spectacle appears to be so contradictory that no room is left for any thought of a possible solution. Put in modern

language, Romeo needs psychic space for deeper develop-
ments and the dawn of new perception, as does the audience.

Such space begins at the opening of Act II (Sc. i, line 2).
Romeo makes his momentous decision: "Turn back, dull
earth, and find thy centre out."

With this self-perceptive remark he reverses his senseless
wandering and scales the wall separating him from the
Capulet orchard.

In this one line we have Shakespeare's message for our
dualistic age. What follows in the second scene is the result of this reversal — the finding of true identity — the
only possible solution of what is so hopelessly contradictory
without it.

Juliet at the window is pouring her heart out to the
stars. She is baffled by the fact that her only love is born of
her only hate, as she has told her nurse. In her case, as in
Romeo's, there has been at first the great wall of contradiction between these opposites.

But now comes the breakthrough made by woman's insight, a typically Shakespearean ordering, as Juliet makes
her .own reversal of perspective and reveals the truth to
Romeo:

> 'Tis but thy name that is my enemy;
> Thou art thyself, though, not a Montague.
>
> Act II, Sc. ii, lines 38-39

(The omission of the comma after the *though* in many
texts has left the line relatively meaningless.)

It is the agency of love at a high, pure level between the
sexes which has made possible this discovery of real identity.
In principle, though in minor degree, this reflects the great
reversals familiar to us in Plato's allegory of the cave,*
where the occupants are told to turn around and face the
sunlight instead of the shadows on the wall, and similarly
in Christ's words on finding one's life by losing the separated self. (Matt.10:39)

Further on in this matchless scene Juliet refers to Romeo's
"gracious self" as the "god" of her idolatry, showing that
beyond the barrier of hate she has truly seen something of

---

* Plato: *The Republic,* Book VII.

the God in him. To widen out the full range of implication
here, we shall be following Shakespeare's lead if we cease
to identify Romeo or our fellow men, including ourselves,
with the whole complex business of outer status or circumstances, such as race, creed, sex, job, political party or nationality. It is not that these natural distinctions should
not exist, but that they should be seen and used as Shakespeare would have them for the enhancement and poetry
of life, not for its warfare and extinction. Unhappily, the
play, read merely as romance, remains one of the world's
most moving but least heeded revealings of the inner path to
peace: the finding of center and identity through widening
circles of love.

The tragedy of accidental mutual death which overtakes
the lovers only adds a final ingredient of conscience to love's
power of healing the breach of rivalry between the warring
houses.

In our nuclear age, when the self-interest of nations is
less and less separable from that of all mankind, the above
extensions of meaning become more and more valid as concrete fact. Their symbolic significance becomes visible as
actuality.

Thus what might appear to be a long step from Romeo's
search for center to Teilhard de Chardin's postulate of the
Omega Point,* or Christ focus, ceases to be merely an in-
triguing speculation. The present curving back of humanity upon itself in a round world may well be the collective
equivalent or outer precursor of the turning of individual
man's consciousness back upon itself in a new perception
of being. Broadly speaking, the plays may be said to anticipate the mutual approach of objective and subjective aspects of reality in man toward the completion of a mighty
circle in his awareness of himself and his planetary existence.

The Mirror Principle

In this introductory chapter it will be well to include a
close look at what is implied by Hamlet's description of

---

* *The Phenomenon of Man*, Pierre Teilhard de Chardin, Harper &
Brothers, New York, 1959.

the intent of drama or "playing." This purpose, he says, "both at the first and now, was and is, to hold as 'twere, the mirror up to nature; to show virtue her own feature, scorn her own image, and the very age and body of the time his form and pressure." *Hamlet* Act III, Sc. ii, lines 23-27. The meaning of the last word is *impression.* Hamlet had been giving instruction to some players to "suit the action to the word, the word to the action" — a principle of exact correspondence between inner and outer processes of life which has a far-reaching significance in all human affairs.

It may be noted also that the author is linking his own sense of the mystery of drama as an instrument of virtue to the great tradition of drama in all ages. The core meaning lies in the fact that as we read, witness, or attempt to live the plays, we ourselves become in a degree our own mirrors of the world. In doing so we draw near to the mystery of all the manifestations of being, the mystery of creation.

Shakespeare's plays, forming in Bacon's phrase "a musical bow of the mind," are extraordinarily rich in the magnetic potency of speech considered as sound, which, according to *The Secret Doctrine** is "the commencement of every manifestation" in the hidden spiritual world. This is why knowledge of the properties and attributes of the idea which is being expressed, together with the properties and attributes of matter, is so important.

It is an understanding of the law of correspondence between these two realms which the whole man needs for his health and harmony of living, and it is here also that the mirror principle, that of reflection, comes in as an indispensable function of the mind. Thus the mirror is infinitely more than a literary device.

The wisdom literature of the world is full of reference to the receptive opening and mirror-like quieting of the mind for this purpose. "Be still and know" is thus a statement of this principle. St. Paul went a step further when he wrote, "But we are all, with unveiled face, reflecting as in a mirror the glory of the Lord, being transformed into the same image from glory to glory." (II Cor. 3:18)

---

* *The Secret Doctrine*, H.P. Blavatsky, Adyar Ed. Vol. I, p. 157. The Theosophical Publishing House, Madras India.

For these reasons Hamlet's description of the purpose of drama as that of holding up a mirror to nature indicates both the exalted purpose of the author and the way the plays are to be approached. The mystery lies in one's inner or universal recognition of identity. Kahlil Gibran has summed up the matter in two lines in *The Prophet*:

> Beauty is eternity gazing at itself in a mirror.
> But you are eternity and you are the mirror.

It was for these same reasons that the Persian Magi carried mirrors as emblems of the material world which reflects Divinity from its every part. As St. Bernard put it, "External nature is but the shadow of God, the soul is His image. The chief, the special mirror in which to see Him is the rational soul finding itself." This refers to the intuition, the simple awareness of pure being, the unconditioned perception — "I exist," or "I am." It is recognition of the fact that consciousness itself is the "Principle which gives life." As Patanjali has stated, "it is the seer standing in his own nature." What we know ordinarily as conscience is also included in the mirror function, as evidenced by Hamlet's use of a play for catching the conscience of a king.

A valuable key to the mysterious role of the mirror principle in the plays is afforded by the following passage from an early essay by Emerson on "Master Minds."

> The way to touch all the springs of wonder in us is to get before our eyes as thought that which we are feeling and doing. The things we do we think not. What I am I cannot describe any more than I can see my eyes. The moment another describes to me the man I am — pictures to me in words that which I was feeling and doing, I am struck with surprise. I am sensible of a keen delight. *I be and see my being at the same time.* If in the "deep instinct of society" I follow another man, it is because he has a part of me, and I follow him that I may acquire myself. (Italics added)

These insights relating to the mirror as a gateway into knowledge of Eternal Man appear to yield the master perspective of the plays. On the basis of these and of other evidences to be considered, Emerson knew himself to be a microcosmic replica of the universe in a process of unfolding which is endless and has no limit. Knowing this as the truth of his own identity as an immortal being and not merely a reasoned external thing, he wished above all to help his fellow men in arriving at a similar vantage point of self-knowledge and adjustment, leading to certainty of their ultimate spiritual kingship.

Chapter II

THE REVOLUTIONARY ROLE
OF THE HEROINES

Portia

The preceding discussion now comes to a point of testing and verification. However, a fundamental shift in focus is necessary if we are to reach through the words and actions of the plays to a further understanding of the one life which lies hidden in them. Our concern in this chapter is with the role assigned to woman in the scheme of human existence, a role capable of filling the void of our modern life when the total nature of her mission is recognized.

It has been truly said that few men have any inkling of what woman really is. This adds a wholly unsuspected dimension to the thesis of Alexis Carrel in his *Man, the Unknown**: that our civilization has been built without a true knowledge of the human being. Among the obvious proofs of both statements is the peril of imbalance and extremism now afflicting our world. The result has been the enormous predominance given to the predatory spirit of material self-interest — the root of conflict and war everywhere. The masculine boast that "this is a man's world" carries with it the seed of that world's destruction. In contrast the Shakespeare plays consistently hold that the qualities of dignity, proportion, beauty and happiness found in any civilization have their source in a psychic and spiritual wholeness-in-duality which the positive and negative principles in each of us require throughout our human span of life.

The divisive, one-sided absolutism of masculine thinking may be illustrated by the following comment of a youth in his teens: "Sex is conquest; love is surrender. Who

---

* Harper & Brothers, New York, 1935.

wants to surrender?" From the Shakespearean point of view verified by history, a civilization is self-doomed to extinction when it loses all sense of the high dignity of sex.

A clear light is thrown on the importance of woman's position in society by the laws of Manu,* the truths of which are exemplified in Shakespeare's heroines. "Where women are honored," says the ancient law-giver, "the gods rejoice; but when they are neglected, all rites and ceremonies are fruitless. Where women grieve, that family quickly perishes. But where women do not grieve, it ever prospers." The implications of this issue in the plays lie too deep and are too decisive to be regarded merely as the work of moralistic speculation.

It is from this standpoint that the potentials of the theater as a school of life are most clearly seen, since the spectator is not being informed or instructed in the ordinary sense, but is left free to interpret what he sees and hears in a manner approximating actual experience. Included in this experience is the way his own mind creates problems by its ordinary dividedness, thus preventing recognition of the wholeness of things. It is in this broad yet intimate sense that the remedial stirring of intuition by the influence of woman, as dramatized by Shakespeare's heroines, may be considered revolutionary for our time. This experience of duality and its transcendence is of fundamental importance, since each person stands or falls as his own actor in his own theater of awareness.

In ancient Indian religions the feminine principle was reverenced as inherent within the cosmic scheme, while the Greeks held a corresponding attitude toward their goddesses. At the level of state affairs, there is meaning for us in Sophocles' portrayal, in Antigone, of the inevitable fall of Creon's rulership when that autocrat, ignoring Antigone's plea to permit the burial of her slain brother in compliance with the symbolic nature rite of her ancestral faith, carries out his threat to contrive her death in a cave.

Thus the polarity of these principles in man is not to be

---

* In Hinduism, the rules of social relationships, based on the Vedas and, according to tradition, given by Manu, the progenitor and first legislator of mankind.

ignored. It is the lesson of history as well as psychology, since nowhere else in our still human nature is the mighty cosmic rhythm between opposites at different levels of consciousness brought to such intense focus, nor with such attendant possibilities of merging at heights of being when exalted feeling is present. The "marriage" of intellect and perceptive feeling, or awareness, is for each individual an indispensable stage in his evolutionary advance. It is in this context that I have singled out Shakespeare's handling of the power of intuition wielded by woman, or the "feminine principle" of consciousness, as an agency of wisdom in the social order.

This integrative factor lies at the heart of the poet's comprehension of the dynamics of human fulfillment. A sustained study of it will throw into relief our modern obsessive fascination with a nihilistic view of life, the work of the separative mind as a slayer of Reality.

The role of Portia in *The Merchant of Venice* calls for particular attention, standing as she does as a triumph of intuition in the midst of the mercantile strife of Venice and, by direct transfer, in the world today. She is the focal point at which the social cruelties of head judgment dissolve in heart wisdom, where mind blends with compassion and reveals the spirit within the letter of the law. The play is the author's major example of the potentials latent in all of us for inner realignments by which manipulative cunning may be converted into justice.

Since Portia is the pivotal character in *The Merchant of Venice* on whom the whole issue turns, everything depends on the way her position is established. She is not an abstraction, but a convincingly feminine person in her own right; yet at the same time she serves a highly symbolic purpose, and it is significant that she is first presented as a prize to be won. Afterwards, when acting in disguise, she is the compassionate interpreter of the law.

In view of the rigid stratification of the religious, economic and social cleavages on which her influence is brought to bear, it is necessary to understand the author's design in weaving together four distinct plots: the "pound of flesh" bond given by Antonio to Shylock when the latter loaned him a sum of money; the elopement of Shylock's daughter, Jessica, with a Christian; the choosing between the three caskets — gold, silver, and lead — by Portia's suitors; and the episode of the betrothal ring.

Bassanio's love for Portia, established early in the play, is used for the occasion of the money problem, since Bassanio goes to his wealthy merchant friend, Antonio, for financial aid. Antonio in turn, with heavy investments at sea, arranges to borrow 3000 ducats from Shylock on the latter's stipulation that if the bond is forfeited, he, Shylock, will be entitled to the satisfaction of cutting a pound of flesh, presumably the heart, from Antonio's body.

Thus the poet-dramatist has woven his web for bringing wisdom into realistic contact with our mortal world. This is the function of the poet, stated in *A Midsummer Night's Dream* as the linking of "heaven and earth" or heart and mind.

The inhumanity of the life-and-death issue over money is emphasized by a reference to the practice of usury which Shylock justified as a natural custom analogous to the breeding of sheep. To liken the increase of the value of money to the propagation of sheep was repugnant to Antonio, who made his money in active trading but charged no interest when making loans. For him, sheep-breeding was on the side of life as a moving, creative principle, distinct by nature from an impersonal system based on mechanical symbols.

We are confronted here with the general direction of a trend in human relations towards either the inclusion or exclusion of the heart-principle, the central issue of the play. Shylock's materialistic hatred of Antonio, which was equal in force to his animosity toward Christians, was based on the fact that Antonio's custom of lending money without charge brought down the rate of interest in the general market.

The intensity of the religious conflict which is reflected in the play is bound up with the economic and social strife and appears in Shylock's parental mortification over the elopement of his daughter, Jessica, with Lorenzo, a Christian gentleman. The emotional ordeal for the father is compounded by Jessica's taking with her a large share of her

father's ducats and jewels, the household having become
for her a "hell," owing to Shylock's penurious "thrift."

By placing the third story, that of the casket scene, in
the middle of the third act, the typical turning point in all
his dramas, Shakespeare establishes the true significance
of Portia not only as Bassanio's bride-to-be, but as embody-
ing the solvent grace and power of the spirit in all human
affairs. The importance of her function is emphasized by
the fact that at the decisive moment when Bassanio is
about to choose, she says:

> I am locked in one of them;
> If you do love me you will find me out.
> > *Act III, Sc. ii, lines 40-41*

Bassanio proves her intuition correct by rejecting the out-
wardly precious caskets and choosing the one of plain lead,
thus proving the triumph of love over self-interest.

> Therefore, then, thou gaudy gold,
> Hard food for Midas, I will none of thee;
> Nor none of thee, thou pale and common drudge
> 'Tween man and man; but thou, thou meagre lead,
> Which rather threat'nest than dost promise aught,
> Thy plainness moves me more than eloquence;
> And here choose I. Joy be the consequence.
> > *Act III, Sc. ii, lines 101-107*

With the story of the betrothal ring added, we see the
interweaving of four main actions, supported by parallels
in secondary actions, as a masterpiece of artistic craftsman-
ship. However, our concern is less with the structural perfection of the play than with the way the author prepares
us for entering the realm of being which he discloses for our
self-testing. Could we succeed in placing ourselves in line
with the axis of wisdom on which everything in the play
turns, we would grasp the reality of its truth and seek to
apply it to our world problem more earnestly than we now
seek sources of power, material advantage, and political and
military ascendancy.

Lest the modern reader regard these statements as an
unwarranted imputing of motives to Shakespeare, it is well
to consider the ancient view of comedy in distinction from

tragedy. A skeptical age, like the present, finds a psychological justification of its mood in posing problems as starkly as possible, leaving the solution to the audience or the reader. On the other hand, the older tradition as represented by the *Book of Job,* Homer's *Odyssey,* the works of Virgil and Dante, the *Arabian Nights,* the vast epics of ancient India, and the romances of medieval Europe, presented the ordeals and vicissitudes of man as having a Promethean value in the growth of self-knowledge and responsibility. The outcome of this view, like that of human evolution itself, was subjective enlightenment attainable by reflective means when applied to the symbolic aspect of all experience. In this sense all such art, including the initiatory rites often reflected in it, recorded the immemorial wisdom tradition concerning the cosmic scheme.

From this standpoint a Shakespearean comedy, especially *The Merchant of Venice,* is not to be taken merely as a contrivance in favor of an optimistic view of life. On the contrary, its testing of human capacity beneath the surface of human events is rigorous in the highest degree. It is from this standpoint that man's creative attitude toward life as focused in Portia is a revolutionary challenge, a call to sanity which today goes unheeded at our peril.

Without an understanding of the details subtly used by the author to establish Portia's real identity early in the play, one is sure to miss the full import of all that follows. In the opening scene Bassanio describes Portia to Antonio as living at Belmont, a place meaning "beautiful mountain." To students of Bible symbolism this indicates the exalted character of seers and prophets, or the quality of wisdom.

In the next line Bassanio emphasizes Portia's beauty as something "fairer" than the ordinary meaning of the word "fair." He is referring to her possession of "wondrous virtues." We then come to a specifically feminine reference: that of the radiant influence of her eyes, which conveyed "fair speechless messages" to Bassanio. (Act I, Sc. ii, lines 162-165) That this implies more than ordinary feminine charm becomes apparent when linked to the crucial casket episode. In other words Bassanio is a lover not only of Portia but of wisdom itself.

This is not, however, to minimize the power of the feminine glance as felt by Bassanio. The "fair speechless messages" were undoubtedly to be taken in a human as well as a symbolic sense. Much of this meaning is conveyed in *Love's Labour's Lost* by Biron's eloquent lines:

> Other slow arts entirely keep the brain
> . . . .
> But love first learned in a ladie's eyes
> Lies not alone immured in the brain,
> But with the motion of all elements
> Courses as swift as thought in every power,
> And gives to every power a double power
> Above their functions and their offices.
> It adds a precious seeing to the eye.
>
> Act IV, Sc. iii, lines 327-333

This is the poet's way of stating the universal fact that just as love inspires the will, so woman, rightly understood and loved, is the inspirer of man. The broad inference to be drawn from this is plain: that an educational system or a civilization which keeps woman confined to the bedroom and the kitchen — in other words regards her activities as exclusively physical — is self-divisive and ends by destroying itself.

These observations serve as an introduction to the testing of Portia's suitors in the casket scenes. It is unfortunate that the meaning of this story has been relegated by a number of scholars and critics to a position of trivial importance. It is even regarded as a "nuisance," something so childishly obvious that it merely gets in the way of the spotlight of dramatic attention trained on the characterization of Antonio and Shylock as their conflict develops. "Of course," runs the argument, "all that glitters is not gold." Why, then, give such importance to the whim of Portia's father in stipulating a choice of caskets for the hand of his daughter, and why place the scene of Bassanio's choosing in the exact middle of the play?

Shakespeare's own answer would seem to be that any surface interpretation of the casket story is bound to be absurd so long as one fails to see what is really at stake. Since the very nature of love is the power to give, and since the reality and meaning of marriage cannot be separated from the reality of our being, it follows that the giving of one's all is the difficult but infinitely rewarding climax of the motive of love. It is the fulfillment of our inborn capacity for union with life which operates within and behind all forms. Obviously this is achievable only after preceding failures at lesser levels of self-giving.

The successive arrangement of the three caskets running counter to the ordinary value structure, places the entire play of *The Merchant of Venice* in immediate relevance to our modern "dilemma of power," just as it did for sixteenth century Europe. Far from being self-evident child's play, the casket story contains in its imagery the scriptural truth of great price: "He that loseth his life for My sake shall find it."

The need for this reversal of our ways of thinking appears in the fact that since the proof of love is the power and will to give rather than possess, the lovers are on trial as to their capacity to love. This whole experience is far removed from romantic emotionalism or sentimentality. Nor is it the result of whim on the part of Portia's aged father.

The reversal signified by the inscription on the lead casket, "Who chooseth me must risk and hazard all he hath," calls for an act of self-knowledge bound up with self-surrender and is therefore rightly the theme of wisdom in all ages. It belongs in the great tradition together with the story of the Prodigal Son, the symbolism of Plato's cave and, in modern science, Teilhard de Chardin's category of the Noosphere in *The Phenomenon of Man* — the advance and centering of humanity's consciousness as it turns round and in upon itself in a round world.

In essence this law of reversal, involving the sacrifice of appearance and false identity to the sustaining principle of being which is behind the mind and belongs to consciousness itself, may be said to be the central motif of Shakespearean drama as a whole. It is the key to play after play, just as it is in a specialized sense for Einstein's physics and the modern proof of non-material reality. Significantly, too, the role of woman as a revolutionary agent of this transformative shifting of awareness comes into clear light in the plays, pointing far ahead to the conscious oneness of humanity in all its diversity — an enormous advance toward harmony with the cosmic order. Measured against Portia and the spiritual meaning of marriage for which she stands, one sees starkly the destruction of potentials for happiness inflicted by our modern exploitation of woman.

Since Bassanio's choice of casket occurs in the middle of the play, and since Portia is the central character throughout, it is appropriate to link with these events the further symbolic fact that the issue of life and death for Antonio is literally the central one of his physical heart, the pound of flesh presumably desired by Shylock. Thus the linkage between man's inner and outer worlds is revealed as the focal point of his destiny, an intimation intended by Shakespeare as the expression of a law of trans-physical geometry in life and art.

It serves to prepare us for the deeply intimate reversal of thinking which the poet was seeking to identify for application to our all too familiar social order. This comes to issue in the trial scene in the fourth act, where the inner law of life, or wholeness, and the outer dictatorship of the head reach open confrontation.

For centuries and especially in recent years the major discussion of the play has revolved around the question of justice meted out to Shylock. The scorn and persecution which he and the Jewish people at large endured at the hands of Christians is faithfully mirrored in Shylock's allusions to his grievances and in Antonio's expression of contempt for Shylock as a person. It is on these lines that a case has been cogently argued in favor of Shylock as a victim of biased treatment.

Due allowance must be made for Shylock's good qualities, even if he has permitted them to be submerged and perverted until he hates Christians, and his attitude toward Antonio is one of ruthless revenge.

Our concern is with the nature of the light thrown on the entire scene of human limitations. Ugliness, disharmony and the bungling of justice in the very midst of efforts to achieve it are seen as an inevitable stage in man's individual growth. Shakespeare's revelation of the anguished twistings and turnings of Shylock's mind under legal testing, especially as the scapegoat for the uneasy conscience of the hard Venetian world, has been said to anticipate Dostoievsky.

From another standpoint a charge of inconsistency, even of playing to the gallery, has been aimed at Portia for her apparent change of tone and manner after delivering her immortal lines beginning,

> The quality of mercy is not strained.
> It droppeth as the gentle rain from heaven
> Upon the place beneath . . .
> Act IV, Sc. i, lines 184-186

Portia had made a good impression of impartiality when, on entering the court and taking up the case, she asked, "Which is the merchant here and which the Jew?" Psychologically this question has been thought to serve a deeper purpose of the author, that of implying that each of the two contestants is unconsciously the alter ego of the other.

The occasion for Portia's eloquent plea for mercy as an ingredient of justice follows immediately after a subtle issue of attitude has been raised when, in reply to Antonio's confirmation of the bond, she declares, "Then must the Jew be merciful," and Shylock instantly challenges her: "On what compulsion must I? Tell me that." (Act IV, Sc. i, lines 112-113)

This raises at once the whole question of the relation of heart to head in all human dealings. Justice in terms of legality and the compulsory enforcement of "law and order" is one thing, but the heart's gift of redemptive mercy is free, as love is, and must come from within. It is there that destiny is ultimately determined. This is the truth of the casket story in another form.

Portia's resort to a relatively cold legality from this point on may be explained by the fact that nothing else can bring home to Shylock the effect and meaning of his rejection of mercy in favor of his vengeful craving of the "law" which sanctioned his intent on Antonio's life. His further rejection of an offer of payment of three times the amount of the bond only underscores his murderous desire.

The charge of a theatrical intent on Portia's part rests chiefly, however, on her holding back the disclosure of two obscure Venetian laws, one against taking a drop of blood and the other against taking the life of a citizen. She keeps these knowingly in reserve until the maximum degree of audience suspense has been reached, despite the fact that Bassanio, who loves her, and Antonio, who has been told to bare his breast for Shylock's knife, are paying a heavy emotional price for this.

The difficulty is to reconcile this charge with Portia's plea for mercy. In other words, it is a question of whether good theater is to be gained at the cost of the principle Shakespeare has embodied in his heroine. One is obliged to look for some middle ground where these apparent opposites might be reconciled.

In defense of Shakespeare, and therefore of Portia, certain overruling considerations should be kept in mind. One is the momentous importance of the issue at stake, involving irrational passions of the intensest kind. In *The Merchant of Venice,* the trial is concentrated within the time and space of a single act. Within these limits one is brought face to face with a multidimensional profundity, the implications of which require such time as is possible for their recognition and absorption.

We see in action the consequences Shylock brings upon himself by rejecting mercy. This is more than an issue of mere legality. It is the law of cause and effect, or karma, made visible.

Portia, however, shows a blended mercy and legal competence when she informs Shylock of the forfeit of goods imposed by law as a penalty for contriving to take the life of another. At the same time she refers the question of Shylock's life to the mercy of the duke. It is because of Shylock's persistently murderous attitude that she concludes her remarks to him with her emphatic, "Down, and beg mercy of the duke," even though Shylock, when the law was against him, had been willing to settle for only his principal.

Turning to Antonio with the question of what act of mercy he could render Shylock, since the relation between the two men was now reversed, she did not expect the outburst of religious prejudice bordering on revenge in Antonio's stipulation that Shylock should become a Christian. The duke had willingly pardoned Shylock his life before he asked it, yet this was intended to impress upon Shylock "the difference of our spirits" as between the Christian and Jewish faiths. This distinction is blurred by Antonio, although his further provision that Shylock bequeath his worldly possessions to Lorenzo and Jessica has in it an element of moral justice.

Any discussion of these subtleties, however, falls away before Shakespeare's central intention: that of holding up the world as a mirror for evoking the spiritual perspective and creativity man needs for transforming his existence. It is Portia's mission in the play to bring about this awakening of spiritual force in the very midst of conditions which brutalize man and make for the death urge.

Portia's influence is always atmospheric, like the music she played prior to Bassanio's choosing of the casket. This has been interpreted as favoritism on her part, but may be quite plausibly regarded as a consistent use of symbolism by the author to suggest Bassanio's natural sensitivity to such things. There was nothing in the worldly character of the two princes — Morocco representing the desire nature and Arragon the mental — to indicate that they had music in their souls or were capable of contact with the higher self.

Such use of music appears as an element of dramatic symbolism in all of the plays and is a self-evident expression of the function of poetical drama which, as previously noted, Bacon quoted "the Ancients" as having termed "the musical bow of the mind." It will be the aim of the chapter on *The Tempest* to extend this meaning to include all of Shakespeare's art as embodied in Ariel.

The Merchant of Venice ends on a sprightly note of complicative action with the ring story, which is introduced at the end of the trial scene. Bassanio, grateful for the young lawyer's handling of the case, asks "him" (Portia) to accept some "remembrance" as a gift, whereupon she insists upon taking his ring. Bassanio refuses, explaining that he was under vow not to sell, give or lose it. After she and her

companion, Nerissa, have left, Bassanio, persuaded by Antonio to reverse his decision, sends the ring after her. In
a brief scene following this, Nerissa in the garb of a lawyer's
clerk adds to the jollity of the situation by planning to
obtain her husband's ring.

The concluding act of the play has but one scene. Significantly this is laid in Portia's garden at Belmont, where
the action serves to restore an engaging naturalness and
femininity to Portia. It also relates the unitary symbolism
of the ring to the resources upon which we may draw when
we dare to blend our minds with the high ultimates of
existence residing in the heart.

Nothing can surpass the exquisiteness of all that this implies when in the silence of a moonlit night Lorenzo and
Jessica sit on a bank and their gaze soars to the wonder and
harmony of the heavens. The music of the spheres to which
Lorenzo refers is the cosmic counterpart and extension of
what man is destined to hear within himself when he has become sufficiently attuned to the song of life.

It is in this context that we may look back briefly to the
events of the casket story, which also occurred at Belmont.
The central relation of that story to everything in the play
and to everything in life places in perspective the revolutionary significance of Shakespeare's vision of the role that is
yet to be played by woman, however far in the future.

Such universal questions as why it is that justice, even the
Statue of Liberty, is represented as a woman, find their
answer in Portia as the living symbol of a new quality of
being which awaits unfoldment when man's mind no longer
denies it or casts a possessive shadow over it, but rather unites
with it to release the creative energy of a supreme wholeness.
Portia is this psychic and spiritual potential, and as such
she acts, though in disguise, as the interpreter of humanity
itself. The court scene serves precisely as an example of how
intuition can function through the disguise or mode of intellect when obliged to play the role of interpreter of the
law in dealing with concrete problems.

In the casket story, as nowhere else in Shakespeare, the
scale of worth in man is clearly and decisively laid bare.
This is no series of judgments passed by others. As each

man chooses, so is he. So also is the fate he brings upon himself at every moment of his life. The self-determined outcomes of action on the part of Antonio and Shylock represent but an extension of this principle.

Thus, in a very real sense, the casket scene makes visible the author's wisdom as well as his art. He does not moralize, but sets human life in motion that it may reveal itself by its own behavior under the spiritual laws which inexorably govern it. Each man thus judges himself by what he thinks and does.

The ending of the play gains an unsuspected force, hidden deep in its poetry, when viewed in this perspective. Accompanying the music, the light of cosmic unity breaks through the screen of our mortal separation and gives us a needed criterion for defining and solving the issues of our lives.

The question of how man can live in harmony with his environment or with his fellow men when not in harmony with himself has grown rapidly more acute with the advance of science and the shrinkage of our world. This means a corresponding increase of importance which the Shakespeare plays have for us.

Ours is an inner choice of caskets. Either we see or do not see the feminine principle of intuition in the makeup of every individual as well as in the consciousness and conscience of mankind. Without this balancing ingredient of creativity and wisdom to round out our intelligence, there can be no harmony. If we do not see what Shakespeare surely intended us to see in Portia, or what Goethe meant when he wrote, "The eternal feminine draws us upward and onward," or what Wagner immortalized in Brunhilde, we consign ourselves to a steadily intensifying meaninglessness of life without a touch of the Holy Spirit, the encourager and inspirer of men.

The creative unity of *The Merchant of Venice*, with its supremacy of heart judgment over that of the head, winds like an ascending stairway up and through a series of crises involving love, discrimination, and justice born of mercy. The poet thus shares with us a glimpse of his own extended vision of man in the higher stages of unfoldment from the human to the cosmic.

How trivial by comparison the moneyed life of man in the little world of Venice suddenly seems with its hard logic of the market place, its rivalries, frustrations and angers! Consider the dreamlike quality of this when all the time man has within himself the means of release from this prison house into a larger and more real freedom of essential being.

Now that the issues of today are increasingly humanistic in the handling of vast material power, one may derive a needed sense of identity and direction from the radiant character of Portia and the widening of spiritual horizons she brings down from her beautiful mountain into our affairs.

Hero

In all of the plays we are constantly standing on the verge of a higher knowledge where the boundaries of ordinary thinking, built into familiar categories by our minds and emotions, fall away and we find we are contained in a larger field of imagination which is yet one with life. We have just seen, for example, that the casket episode in *The Merchant of Venice* is more than childish fantasy, since the decisions involved reflect realities hidden in all human experience. What is mirrored is the mystery of unity, the key to the whole play.

In tracing the revolutionary implications of the emergence of man into a new quality of being, the specific attention given to the agency of woman falls into place as a conspicuously dramatic element. Broadly speaking, this feminine influence adds indispensably not only to the poetry, but to a profoundly psychosynthetic atmosphere of growth.

A striking case of the sudden dispersal of illusion by insight is afforded by Hero, the bride-to-be, in *Much Ado About Nothing*. Don John, the villain, has contrived a plot for preventing the marriage of Hero and Claudio, whom he hates. He has arranged to have Claudio witness and overhear a night-time scene in which one of Hero's waiting-maids, impersonating Hero, is wooed by one of Don John's followers at Hero's chamber window. Claudio, believing what he sees as evidence of Hero's unfaithfulness, is determined to shame her publicly the next morning at the time set for the wedding.

When the moment of ceremonial union arrives, Claudio rejects Hero as "a rotten orange" and interprets her blush as proof of guilt. He has just chided Hero's father, Leonato, for daring to vouch for his, Claudio's, absence of any objection to the marriage, adding a word of contempt for men who daily act without knowing what they do. The irony of this remark as applying to Claudio himself gains point as he challenges Hero to declare the name of the man who had talked with her at her window the night before. When she denies talking with any man, Don Pedro confirms the false charge on the strength of what he, together with Don John, and Claudio, had seen.

The buildup of illusion reaches its climactic force when, finally, Claudio taunts Hero on the meaning of her name, and her father wishes his own death at the hand of some man with a dagger. Hero swoons, stricken by the unbearable force of false accusation.

Instantly the situation takes on a new perspective and another order of experience begins. At this point the meaning of the word "Nothing" in the title of the play suddenly assumes a reversed significance. In the case of Hero and Claudio it transforms everything. The friar, who was to conduct the wedding, becomes an agent of nature and an ally of the unconscious in Hero by gaining her father's consent to permit a temporary hiding away of his daughter on the pretext that she is dead. He even recommends a show of burial rites. His intent is to change Claudio's slanderous attitude toward Hero into remorse, and still more, to allow "the idea of her life" to work on his imagination in such a way as to endear her to him beyond anything he had previously known.

Since Leonato is more than willing, the friar counsels Hero, who has revived, with the words:

> Come, lady, die to live; this wedding day
> Perhaps is but prolonged; have patience and endure.
> > Act IV, Sc. i, lines 255-256

Here speaks the immemorial wisdom. The law of transi-

tion, both natural and spiritual, moves from a given state of
conditionedness to a relatively new and greater life through
the gateway of death. The friar condenses into three words
what he has just referred to as "the strange course" he is
pursuing in order that through "travail" he might bring
about a "greater birth." The traditional meaning behind
the expression, "Die to live," is that the right way of solving
any problem is to be found only at a level of insight above,
beyond or within the outer form in which the problem
appears.

J. Krishnamurti makes a comparable statement that to
die to every experience every minute is to live totally in an
altogether different dimension. In other words, to truly
know a thing one must transcend it. As applied to self-
knowledge, the seeker of wisdom must "die" to, or stand
free of, his own form-bound egoism, his illusory identification with appearances, the conditioning which, unknown
to himself, he habitually imposes on his awareness of everything, including himself, thus totally obscuring his perception of the Universal Life or Self in him and in all else.

Claudio's lesson is not finished until the final act of the
play, when again he has to surmount the trial of appearances. This time it is by an act of humility and faith.
When the whole story of Don John's evil deception is
brought to light after his men have been captured, Claudio
begs forgiveness of Leonato. This he is granted on condition that he marry the latter's niece, whose face he has not
seen and may not see until after the wedding, but whom
Leonato described as resembling Hero.

Claudio, believing that Hero has died, agrees and in so
doing brings into action the higher part of his nature, a
surrender of self somewhat akin to that of Bassanio in choosing Portia's casket. The fact that he has not seen the girl's
face is symbolic, since he had not truly fathomed the character of Hero, a matter which love itself or his own intuition should have taught him.

After the wedding ceremony Claudio rejoices on discovering that his bride is Hero. Thus the only "death" is
that of Claudio's illusion. It is with the need to discover the
untruth or nothingness of one's illusions that the "much

ado" of the characters is concerned.

In this play Hero is the passive agent rather than, like Portia, the active exemplar of the wisdom principle Shakespeare ascribes to many of his heroines. Nevertheless the fact goes to prove the range of the author's purpose and artistic strategy as he holds up to mankind a mirror of the archetypal quality he felt the Claudios, Moroccos, and Arragons, as well as others, need to discover about the true nature of woman and her destined part in the redemption of society.

Cordelia

In *King Lear,* a play regarded as the greatest example of sustained creative energy in all literature, the action turns upon the King's relation to his youngest and favorite daughter, Cordelia. The storm of his outraged arrogance of power is set in motion at the opening of the play by one word, "Nothing." This is Cordelia's answer when commanded to measure her love for her father in words he expects to be still more fulsomely flattering to him than that of Goneril and Regan. Hearing their false protestations of love, she had concluded that her only recourse was to "love and be silent."

When she repeats the word, "Nothing," in reply to her father's further insistence, he declares that "Nothing will come of nothing" and thereby reveals his ignorance both of Cordelia's love and of life's inner reality. To him her silence is but empty, obstinate negation.

The rest of the play is the ordeal of Lear's initiation into these meanings, an outcome made possible only by living through the adversity he had brought upon himself. It is the answer to the enigma of the world's suffering today.

Lear, as his own "angry ape," can emerge finally and stand in his own true nature as "glassy essence" only by breaking out of his habitual reactions, in this case his tyrannical vanity. This is what Kent, the king's faithful guide and mentor, had in mind when he spoke three fateful words: "See better, Lear." The accent is almost that of the oriental mystic, Patanjali. To bring about this change in

himself, Lear must die to his egoism and learn compassion
at the price of his own agony. It is for the crowning of
his struggle and his true kingship that Cordelia's love reenters the play during the final scenes.

This play offers special opportunity for identifying and
tracing the signs and tokens of the great prophetic tradition
which is the spiritual substance underlying all of the plays.
Cordelia's love for her father and his for her cannot be regarded as merely romantic or sentimental. Hence its power,
tested by all the extremities of Lear's injured vanity and the
vicissitudes of age as well as of political fortune, cannot be
interpreted as other than it is: a major redemptive force
wielded by the feminine principle in life when that principle is deeply true to itself. It is under such circumstances
that Shakespeare brings us face to face with a reality which
the tempests of life only reveal the more convincingly, and
we find ourselves dealing with something incommensurable
in the midst of particulars.

Unknowingly, Lear has been as self-interested and petty
as his two older daughters. They serve as mirrors of this
quality in himself, and by the humiliation they bring upon
him, he is obliged to distinguish true from false love. In
addition, the test tears away everything he thought himself
to be and shakes him to the verge of madness, just as earlier
the blinded Earl of Gloucester is allowed to hover for a
moment on the brink of suicide at Dover cliff.

In the middle of the play, as always, we come to the
turning point. Lear defies the powers of the storm yet
accepts them without rancor, humbly acknowledging himself, in his self-pity, to be only "A poor, infirm, weak and
despised old man." It has taken the superior force of nature's elements to bring about this humbling, but it is a
necessary beginning. The encasing shell of his identification
with status has been cracked, and from here the experience
works its psychological effect inwardly.

The reversal of his attitude is strikingly indicated at
once by his resolve: "No. I will be the pattern of all
patience. I will say nothing." This last word takes us back
at once to the original issue of *nothingness* which alienated
him from Cordelia. We recall in new perspective the wrath-

ful decision he brought down upon her as a threat: "thy truth, then, be thy dower," when he revoked his plan to bestow on her the fairest portion of his estate.

Now, however, the realized nothingness of his own separated personality becomes the source of his ecstasy of reunion with her. We have here the mystical salvation theme of the great religions. The "truth" which Lear in his spiritual blindness had decreed as Cordelia's dower is the love she had known all along, despite his limitations. For him, at the time, this had been only a negation, an emptiness, a denial of the false thing he had demanded; but now it proves to be a fulfillment.

The absoluteness of Lear's present reversal together with the illumination it throws forward to the ending of the play, appears in starkest vividness when we remember the terible oath with which he sought to confirm his decision to ban Cordelia from his life:

> For, by the sacred radiance of the sun,
> The mysteries of Hecate and the night,
> By all the operation of the orbs
> From whom we do exist, and cease to be;
> Here I disclaim all my parental care,
> Propinquity of property and blood,
> And as a stranger to my heart and me
> Hold thee, from this, for ever.
>
> Act I, Sc. i, lines 111-118

Such an oath, binding the king to the process of the cosmic order itself, could result only in an extremity of humiliation and personal defeat at the hands of those same forces. This is karma, or cause and effect, in its most elemental form. Yet the irate king's disclaimer of all future ties which hiddenly and unbrokenly united him to Cordelia proved to be the actual "nothing" when he was prepared by suffering to enter the realm of being where true kingship resides.

In the hovel scene of Act III, where the human setting is narrowed down to the humblest dimension, the point of order in entering the hovel is settled by Lear when, on being invited to go first, he defers in favor of the fool — "you houseless poverty," he calls him.

The next lines come spontaneously from his now opened heart:

> Poor naked wretches, whereso'er you are
>
> . . . .
>
> How shall your houseless heads and unfed sides,
> Your loop'd and window'd raggedness, defend you
> From seasons such as these?

Then comes Lear's great confession of self-discovery:

> . . . . O, I have ta'en
> Too little care of this! Take physic, pomp;
> Expose thyself to feel what wretches feel,
> That thou may'st shake the superflux to them
> And show the heavens more just.
>
> Act III, Sc. iv, lines 28-36

When Edgar enters the hovel disguised as a madman — another self-mirror for Lear — and tells an imaginary tale of his own deeds of pride and false dealing and the extremity to which these have brought him, Lear strips off his own clothing and thus symbolically as well as actually confronts the eternal question of what man is.

The inner battle between newly awakened compassionate patience and the former fury is not yet completely won, but continues in Act IV. Yet in the last scene the transformation proceeds during a sleep of exhaustion into which the king falls.

Meanwhile French forces supporting Cordelia's cause have landed with her and set up camp at Dover. Learning of Lear's condition, she arranges for his being brought to her. At the same time she prays that the "kind gods" or powers of healing bring to harmony "the untuned and jarring senses" of her "child-changed father." How significant the phrase, reminding one of the scriptural admonition to become as "a little child."

In this phrasing the whole secret of spiritual as well as physical restoration is suggested, a process symbolized by the fact that a gentleman attendant has clothed the sleeping king in fresh garments. Not only this, but he called for louder music, thus literally translating into action Cordelia's metaphorical language.

Portia also made use of music at the time of Bassanio's choosing of the casket. Again we see the power of musical or poetical speech which prevails in all of the plays as an atmospheric influence for the growth and healing of mankind.

This principle, it may be added parenthetically, was familiar to Lord Bacon and appears in what Shelley recognized as his poetical style, a circumstance which gains significance from the fact that Bacon had a statue of Orpheus on his estate at Verulam. The latter name, furthermore, is said to have been derived from the Latin designation of the stream — the "river of truth" — which flowed through the original Roman settlement at that spot. In point of symbolic suggestiveness nothing could apply more appropriately to the inexhaustible flow of consciousness, the *atmic* stream of truth and being, which winds through the plays.

The kiss which Cordelia gives her sleeping father tells the story of a love so real that it conquers all things. It is the seal of the "truth" which Lear in his anger had rejected.

When the king awakes, he first chides Cordelia for taking him out of the grave. He regards himself still "bound upon a wheel of fire," the mental torture through which he has come. In answer to Cordelia's question if he *knows* her, he calls her a spirit, at the same time wondering when she had died.

Such, then, is the theme of "die to live," the key to *Much Ado About Nothing,* reappearing in a new and far more intensely dramatic form. The story is Promethean in this respect.

As Lear painfully gropes his way back to a recollection of where he is, he asks his attendant gentleman to bless him, and when the latter attempts to kneel in performing the benediction, the king forbids the action, thinking the man is mocking him. He thinks of himself now as reduced to the condition of "a very foolish fond old man." (Act IV, Sc. vii, line 60.) This is true humility, not self-pity.

At this point it dawns on Lear that Cordelia is his child. Yet he wants to know if her tears are real and offers to drink poison if she will give it to him, since she is still

identified in his mind with the evil spirit of his two elder
daughters.

When he asks if he is now in France, Kent assures him
in the language of a seer: "In your kingdom, sir." (Act IV,
Sc. vii, line 76.) His meaning is only indirectly geographical,
since he is referring to Lear's kingdom of the mind.

Lear's last words in this critical scene are to "forget and
forgive." (Act IV, Sc. vii, line 84.) He has passed through
the ordeal of his illusions and is ready to discover beyond
all doubt the dignity, even divinity, of the love Cordelia has
held for him unbrokenly. Forgiveness opens the door to
self-change, just as it is the initial key to effecting improvement in all human affairs.

In the brief second scene of Act V, Edgar announces to
his father that the king's army has been defeated and Cordelia captured. Noting his father's reluctance to move, he
urges patience:

> Men must endure
> Their going hence, even as their coming hither:
> Ripeness is all.
>
> Act V, Sc. ii, line 11

The wisdom condensed in the last three words can cover
the whole play and beyond, including the cosmic life-proc-
ess itself. As for human relations, it points to the eventually rounded symmetry of each man's qualities in relation to
himself, a condition which carries wholeness with it in his
adjustment to others and to the race.

In the tremendous final scene (Act V. Sc. iii) Lear invites Cordelia to come away with him to prison. There they
will "sing like birds" in the cage of their finite limitations
because love has transcended these. From the vantage point
of what he calls "the mystery of things" — a perfect description of the realm of being they have entered together —
they will behold the ruling of universal truth or law behind particular events "as if we were God's spies," and the
ups and downs of political fortune will be no more perma-
nently binding or important than the alternating moon-gov-
erned tides of the sea.

Lear's attainment of the power to "see better" is now
all but completed. Yet one more step remains. This is

when he is confronted with the death of Cordelia at the hands of Edmund, the Earl of Gloucester's illegitimate son. The death of the two other sisters is the work of Goneril who, in jealousy over Regan's love for Edmund, poisons her and then stabs herself.

This leaves Lear, the sole remnant of his family, to endure the deepest of his sufferings alone. Goneril and Regan have loved their father for what they could get. Cordelia alone loved him for himself. It required the whole ordeal of the play for him to learn the difference by discovering the secret in his own heart. It is all an intimate parable of the world experience today.

Commensurate with Lear's final agony is the triumph of his vision in the closing lines. Against the utter pathos of his lament, "And my poor fool is hang'd," and the re-iterated finality of his conclusion that Cordelia will never come again, he exclaims with his own dying breath, "Look there, look there," as if he were gazing past the imagined movement of her lips and saw beyond death itself.

These closing events reveal most poignantly the degree of vision Lear had attained, through suffering, in learning to "see better." They accord with the well known fact that a voluntary recognition and acceptance of one's condition is a gateway to release, an uncovering of awareness of the perceiving principle itself which is unconditioned, namely, consciousness *per se.* Through this voluntary confrontation lies the path to freedom. This is the teaching provided by the ancient mystery schools so often shunned when viewed externally as a kind of prison. It is pertinent to recall that Dante's route of release from hell was through the middle of it; that is, by a direct facing and acceptance of fact, beyond which lies the unconditioned.

Thus Lear, as mental man, symbolically accompanied by Cordelia, the inspirer of his intuition, achieves "rightness" of understanding. Herein we see the revolutionary role of woman in the plays reflecting the mystery of unity that is in nature. When Lear dies, it is not in a state of defeat as usually interpreted on the stage, but one of victory and ecstasy. In death he has taken upon him the mystery of eternal life.

In this connection, as in that of the formula "die to live," examined previously, Keats' penetrating insight that "Shakespeare lived a life of allegory and his works were his commentary on it" has striking confirmation. To grasp the truth of this we have only to read the whole of Shakespeare's 146th sonnet:

> Poor soul, the centre of my sinful earth,
> Fool'd by these rebel powers that thee array
> Why dost thou pine within, and suffer dearth
> Painting thy outward walls so costly gay?
> Why so large cost, having so short a lease,
> Dost thou upon thy fading mansion spend?
> Shall worms, inheritors of this excess,
> Eat up thy charge? Is this the body's end?
> Then, soul, live thou upon thy servant's loss,
> And let that pine to aggravate thy store;
> Buy terms divine in selling hours of dross,
> Within be fed, without be rich no more.
> So shalt thou feed on death that feeds on men,
> And, Death once dead, there's no more dying then.

Nothing could be more inevitable than that a man of such comprehensive vision should dramatize in a spirit of creativity and play this supreme reversal of man's awareness of himself, especially upon entering and treading the way of inward unfoldment laid down by nature and by mystical science in all ages.

Rosalind

We now pass to a further instance of Shakespeare's use of his heroines as types of a needed revolutionary force in society.

In *As You Like It,* Rosalind is the life of the play because of her balance of qualities. In her complete naturalness under all circumstances her love sparkles as wisdom, and her wisdom is radiant with love. According to the most ancient definition of philosophy, the one cited in H. P. Blavatsky's *The Secret Doctrine,* (Adyar Ed. 1938, Vol. V, p. 265, footnote) the word originally meant not the love of wisdom, but the wisdom of love. That is, the first impulse attributed to Brahman in breathing forth the universe is the will to multiply — not in the sense of external expansion, but of qualitative variation and richness within the One.

At the human level, Rosalind is Shakespeare's unique agent of love, in the sense of being equally at home in society and in the forest of Arden. There she serves as a reconciler between our human opposites of sophistication and simplicity.

Beneath the veil of delightful Arcadian phantasy, the spirit of Rosalind lives as something authentic in its own right, the concrete yet symbolic expression of a wholeness and meaning in life which leads to the solution of a multitude of our man-made ills.

It is beside the point to hold that the play is too remote or fanciful in conception and tone to have a real bearing on the self-alienation with which we afflict ourselves today. We are mistaken in accepting the play only as a charming example of the poet's fling at Utopian escapism, reasoning as we do that the circumstances of the setting are no longer possible and that a symbolic interpretation is too far out to be convincing.

The question at issue here is the perennial one: that of the good life and how to live it on terms inherent in life itself and the total order of things. At all times and under all circumstances the type of civilization man creates for himself is subject to the laws of proportion and balance existing equally in nature and in man. Thus the old duke confides that he draws instruction from his own adversity and, in the tradition of all sages,

> Finds tongues in trees, books in the running brooks,
> Sermons in stones and good in everything.
>
> Act II, Sc. i, lines 16-17

This is the voice of wisdom, the realm of being, the central theme or principle of the play. Rosalind exemplifies it in her feminine manner by converting or "translating" the "stubbornness of fortune" into opportunity for the triumph of the human spirit as it unfolds from within and utilizes all circumstances for building up its remedial power of perception. As an embodiment of romance in this meaningful sense, Rosalind is a universal image of woman.

From this standpoint the play is an allegory of how each of us may live his life with enough directness, simplicity and imagination to correct his own bias. It throws into relief the distorting influence of the prejudices and artificialities, the emptiness and boredom which thrive today in a society dangerously at odds with the unity both of nature and mankind.

Rosalind, disguised as a boy, is a vehicle of sanity which blends masculine and feminine qualities of wit and love. For these reasons she is the personification of an art of living which is revolutionary when applied to a sick world like ours, which has rapidly been losing its knowledge of how to find, even to seek, the wisdom it needs for its own healing. If one agrees that the object of all mature thinking is a wise point of view and that the test of all experience lies in the transformation of one's own being as life goes on, it follows that the role of Rosalind as a human type has permanent significance for our understanding of the ends of life as more important than the means. Disaster follows when this order is reversed and the means become forces creating their own ends.

A few further reflections on the scheme of the play, with Rosalind in the middle, may be suggestive. The emphasis given to life lived in a natural setting should be regarded as in line with the purpose of all the plays, that of complete living. Herbert Spencer used this phrase in describing the purpose of education. The act of changing ourselves and our ways of thinking to accord more and more fully with this rounding out of our potentials constitutes the real growth-objective of Shakespearean drama, as it does of life itself. As soon as this principle is understood, it sets in motion a regeneration force field within us which is capable of rendering everything in life significant.

What may appear to be merely fanciful in the setting and circumstances of Rosalind's world is designed to open our imagination sufficiently for entering a pathway of self-change, thus providing leverage for changing our actual world and its ways of thinking.

This calls for a close but free investigation of all the particulars which the poet has playfully assembled to reveal the theme of human regeneration. He is inviting us to move in imagination with the refining process he has set in motion through the willingness of the characters to give up the illusions of which they have been victims in their self-ignorance. It is the theme of "die to live" in a new form, this time with man's understanding of his relation to nature as the solvent of the problems he brings upon himself in his state of separation from the total order.

All of this may strike us as fanciful and unreal because we are alienated from it by the conditioning we have imposed on ourselves in our superficial and divisive civilization. As a result the mind of modern man is no longer "fresh, clear, innocent — a light to itself," as J. Krishnamurti is constantly reminding us. For the sake of business, many people sell themselves, put up false fronts, and stifle all sense of their relation to the flow of consciousness which pervades and upholds existence — a world of which, as Bacon wrote, our knowledge should be the image.

The skepticism which rejects the "back-to-nature" thesis as a quaintly picturesque but outworn bit of sentimentality prevents our grasping the central implications of Shakespeare's design: that of the cosmic law for man which is inherent in the total stuff of which he, a microcosm, is made. The average city dweller, caught in the wheels of mechanized life, wishes secretly to "get away from it all," yet surrenders to the system by concluding that "someone must keep the wheels turning."

The role of Rosalind in *As You Like It* is revolutionary in the sense of winning us away from our acceptance of artificiality as something to which we must inevitably surrender. She incarnates the freedom of naturalness to the extent that we are capable of responding, frees us from the feeling of guilt, despair and boredom which hangs over our way of life like a cloud and excludes us from any true understanding of life and love. The revolt of modern youth in its truest motivation is a painful, often devious groping toward the resilient spirit of complete and balanced living which Rosalind embodies.

She is convincing not because of her charm; she represents a principle immanent in the universe. She is a challenge to those who are not happy with present existence — a challenge not proved by logic, but one that is understood and made admirable by feeling. She is an instrument in the poet's hands for destroying man's image of himself as a separated person and restoring him to a life keyed to a more total reality and therefore triumphant over adversity.

The spirit of the play is voiced at the end of the first act when Rosalind, banished from Duke Frederick's court and accompanied by her cousin Celia, departs with the defiant affirmation:

> Now go we in content
> To liberty and not to banishment.
> Act I, Sc. iii, lines 139-140

A new mind, the making of a new world, is emerging in the two girls because they dare to be themselves, a fact significant because it means something far more than a mere reaction against authority.

Viola

In *Twelfth Night* Viola plays a role comparable to that of Rosalind as the restorer of a natural wholeness and meaning to life. The problem is similarly "modern," although developed from another angle.

Here the setting, likewise the problem, is suggested by the name of the locality, Illyria, suggesting illusion. Something is amiss at Duke Orsino's court, and the subtle psychological character of what is wrong appears in the opening of the play. Not love itself, which is a giving forth, but the "appetite of it," the desire of self to feed emotionally on sensation to a point "of excess and surfeit," especially when stimulated by music, is the thing which tantalizes him and renders his life unsatisfying, illusory, "fantastical." This is the leading symptom of a sickness or imbalance. It is the Illyrian quality of the society into which Viola enters as a ray of healing light at the beginning of the second scene.

Her arrival in this strange land is a surprise to her, the result of a shipwreck from which she was rescued, but in which her twin brother, Sebastian, was allegedly drowned. As Harold Goddard points out in his *The Meaning of Shakespeare*, Sebastian is therefore associated in her mind with a higher world, that of Elysium — an association appearing in all that Viola comes to represent as an influence in the play. She is the intuitive power of woman, the rectifying force of true love, although necessarily acting in disguise as a page at the duke's court. She is the inspiring principle which the mind needs for its illumination and the guidance of society.

It will be helpful at this point to consider more specifically than heretofore the law of polarity which at all times governs Shakespeare's symbolic use of his heroines, especially when presented in disguise. Here a hidden factor becomes operative. In Lear's words, "we take upon's the mystery of things."

As in the world today, what has to be accomplished in Illyria is the healing of a sick community. In both instances we are looking into the drama of a curative process which exists in nature but requires, as in depth psychology, a quality of administering made possible by an imaginative merging of science and art. The play points ahead to our modern problem of coping with the imbalances, outer and inner, which lead to violence. This, for Shakespeare, is the center of mutual reference which exists between the man and the woman, or intellect and intuition, in each of us, where the secret of total meaning lies.

This is the mission of Viola, not only in her role as a page, but in her relation to her brother Sebastian. In her the restorative power of an Elysian principle is at work inter-threading human relations with lines of love, imagination, self-honesty, and a vision of confident surrender to the needs and processes of inner change.

The buffoonery of Toby Belch, Andrew Aguecheek and Malvolio seems exactly calculated to serve as a foil to this. Taken together these opposites of insight and stupidity define a human need existing behind appearances, where intuition conceals yet ultimately reveals a wisdom capable of saving the Illyrian community from moral drowning. The Shakespearean theme is centered in the redemptive side of

Viola's identity, biding its time until the final moment of
revelation permitting her marriage to the duke.

Indeed, to cite once more Edgar's observation in *King
Lear,* "ripeness is all." It applies to the blending of man's
faculties at such time as they are quantitatively and qualita-
tively mature. Without exception the entire rhythmic movement of life in the plays is designed for this maturing.

Hermione and Perdita

Beyond illustrating the nature and unfoldment of being
as revealed by Shakespeare, no attempt has been made in
these discussions to formulate a rule of thumb for explaining
life's mysteries, as if such a thing were possible. Instead,
what is sought is a quality of feeling and insight which may
serve to deepen one's appreciation of the poet's use of history and folk tales in relating the creative function of art
to man's discovery of his inner world.

A further example of this is drawn from ancient myth as
it lends itself to the poet's purpose in *The Winter's Tale.*
For the main idea of a direct linkage of this play to sources
in the Eleusinian Mysteries, the writer is indebted to a work
by W. F. C. Wigston entitled *Bacon, Shakespeare and the
Rosicrucians,* published in 1888.

It is necessary to sketch the plot of the play briefly. The
action which precipitates the initial problem, the separation
between King Leontes and his queen, Hermione, with the
attendant loss of their daughter, Perdita, is the result of a
deranging fit of jealousy which overtakes the king during a
visit of his lifelong friend Polixenes, king of Bohemia. The
open cordiality of the queen is misinterpreted by Leontes.
Camillo, a faithful courtier, on being instructed by Leontes
to poison Polixenes, but knowing the latter to be innocent,
warns him of the danger and offers to accompany him on an
immediate escape to Bohemia.

This flight so confirms Leontes' suspicion that he has
his wife imprisoned and, openly accusing her of infidelity,
he declares that her baby soon to be born is the child of
Polixenes. At the birth of a girl, Leontes orders the infant
removed to a distant land.

In the third act Hermione is placed on public trial. A favorable turning point occurs, however, on the arrival of a message from the Oracle of Apollo at Delphos declaring, "Hermione is chaste; Polixenes blameless; Camillo a true subject; Leontes a jealous tyrant; his innocent babe truly begotten; and the king shall live without an heir if that which is lost be not found." (Act III, Sc. ii. lines 132-137.) The rest of the play consists in the restoration of Hermione and the finding of the lost daughter, Perdita.

The theme of the present discussion is the part played by woman in rectifying the imbalance of a man-made world in which the universal law of the polarity of opposites in the oneness of life is tragically ignored.

The title, *The Winter's Tale,* is linked to the Greek myth of the cyclic death and rebirth of earth life represented by the annual change from winter to spring and summer. In Shakespeare's handling, as in the mysteries of Eleusis, this cycle, storied in the myth of Demeter (or Ceres) and Persephone (Proserpina), is a cosmic prototype of the relation of death to life in the physical and spiritual experience of man. The details of this analogy in the play are unmistakable, as is their relevance to Shakespeare's vision of his art in relation to nature.

The swiftly moving events in Act III include the fainting and the apparent death of Hermione on hearing the verdict of the Oracle of Apollo, followed by the news that Leontes' son, Mamillius, has died of grief over the desperate plight of his mother. Meanwhile the infant girl, Perdita, who has been left unprotected on the shore of Bohemia, is found by an old shepherd.

In Act IV, after a lapse of sixteen years, Polixenes learns that his son, Florizel, is in love with a shepherd girl (Perdita) of unknown parentage, and goes in disguise to investigate. On learning that the betrothal is about to occur, the king discloses his own identity and that of his son and stops the proceeding. Camillo, however, has been so charmed by Perdita's beauty and dignity that he urges her and Florizel to go on an immediate visit to Sicily and present themselves to Leontes.

Act V then brings the story back to the court of Leontes,

who welcomes Florizel and Perdita. Polixenes speedily arrives also, as well as Camillo, and in the rapid succession
of events the emotions of Leontes are torn by extremes of
joy and sorrow and a final return to happiness. A mysterious
box brought by the shepherd is opened, disclosing Perdita's
baby clothes and jewels as proof of her identity as the king's
lost daughter. Leontes is further elated over Perdita's betrothal to the son of his old friend, Polixenes, but is de-
pressed by remembrance of Queen Hermione's alleged death.
Unknown to him she had remained in seclusion, refusing
to be known as alive until her daughter should be restored.

The scene which ends the play is a work of striking symbolism, rendering unmistakable the linkage of the play's
meaning to the ancient mystery teachings of the Greeks relating to the cosmic law that the rebirth or renewal of life
is through seeming death. *Mors janua vitae* — death is the
gateway of life — conveys the meaning in a Roman saying.

Paulina, wife of one of the court lords, has been Hermione's protectress through the long wintry season of her grief
and seeming death. She has guarded the secrecy of Hermione's disappearance and created an impression that she has
caused a lifelike statue of her to be made.

The summit of the play's theme is reached when, in a
chapel in her house, Paulina draws aside a curtain and reveals the "statue" to the assembled chief characters. Leontes
is struck by remorse, the more so because the silent figure
reminds him of Hermione's majesty of bearing and her patient tenderness and absence of chiding. At the same moment
Polixenes notes an appearance of warmth on Hermione's
lips, and Leontes exclaims:

> The fixture of her eye has motion in't,
> As we are mocked with art.
> > Act V, Sc. iii, lines 67-68

The return of life to a seemingly lifeless statue is given
emotional intensity for Leontes by the gradual transition.
Paulina offers to close the curtain again, but Leontes is so
fascinated by the thought of an imminent return of life to
the image of Hermione that he begs Paulina to allow him
twenty years for dwelling on such an anticipation:

> No settled senses of the world can match
> The pleasures of that madness.
> > Act V, Sc. iii, lines 72-73

When he wishes to kiss the statue, Paulina restrains him, but promises "more amazement" if he is ready to behold what is still to be revealed: the actual life and movement of the statue.

Psychologically the moment of revelation is carefully prepared, as indicated by Paulina's announcement:

> It is required
> You do await your fate.
> > Act V, Sc. iii, lines 94-95

There is a brief silence during which Paulina insists on the departure of any adversely minded person. Then significantly she calls for music as she directs the statue to descend from the platform.

The restoring of life to a statue of seeming death is described by Paulina as a work of natural law and therefore "holy." Leontes in turn says:

> If this be magic, let it be an art
> Lawful as eating.
> > Act V, Sc. iii, lines 110-111

At this moment Paulina, announcing to Hermione that Perdita has been found, summons the latter to kneel before her mother and ask her blessing. She then joyfully invites these two "precious winners" to "go together" and share their exultation with everyone.

Leontes ends the play by asking pardon for his original suspicion, adding the final directive that

> Each one demands an answer to his part
> Perform'd in this wide gap of time since first
> We were dissever'd.
> > Act V, Sc. iii, lines 153-155

With the essential features of the plot now before us, we may look into the patterning of their symbolism around the central theme, that of the restoration of life from apparent death. We see repeated the relation of death to life

which, in the formula of "die to live," marks the upturn in
the fate of Hero in *Much Ado About Nothing*. In terms of
the nature process associated in *The Winter's Tale* with
gardening and the growth of flowers, we are justified in
linking the same principle to the analogy drawn by Jesus
between the necessary "death" of the seed in the ground
and that of man's material selfhood relative to his spiritual
birth.

Yet the chief and all but literal frame of reference in the
play is that known throughout classical antiquity as the
relation between Demeter and her daughter Persephone,
or Ceres and Proserpina. In its obvious nature symbolism
the myth refers to the cycle of the seasons, specifically to
the life-giving return after winter of spring, summer and
autumn. Perdita is the lost daughter whose separation from
her mother, Hermione, was caused by the separation of
Leontes and Hermione, a breach which could be healed only
by the finding of Perdita, as stated by the oracle.

At this point the dramatist's close identification of Perdita with the love and cultivation of flowers becomes significant — a fact which also indicates the author's love of
gardens. In a sense Perdita's life was a human flowering of
the seasonal qualities revealed in the plant world, since
she had been brought up away from the courts in a natural
environment where she could grow as the flower grows —
spontaneously. She is Rosalind and Viola over again at a
level where the blending of humanity and nature can be
felt as a life process working in us from birth. Perdita is
the spirit of new life, the rebirth of nature's creativity, after
the deathlike state of winter and, by analogy, after all the
freezings or artificial fixations which man imposes on his
states of existence.

Little wonder that Perdita, like the poet-author, operates
as an agent of nature itself and is to be understood as one
of nature's creators. Nor is it by chance that the philosophy
of this symbolism should appear in a famous passage in
Act IV describing the relation of art to nature.

Nowhere in literature is this relationship more pointedly
or more appealingly linked by symbolism to our racial wisdom. Polixenes is enlarging on the subject of flower grow-

ing which Perdita has introduced, particularly the role of human skill in furthering nature's design. He makes the point that even this skill or art has its cosmic origin, for

> . . . Nature is made better by no mean
> But nature makes that mean: so, ever that art
> Which you say adds to nature, is an art
> That nature makes.
>
> Act IV, Sc. iv, lines 89-92

Admittedly the crossing of flower stocks or species brings about an improvement, or at least a change, but "The art itself is nature."

Here the voice of the author is speaking for mankind's acknowledgment of our creative kinship with the universe through art. More specifically, in the exquisite lines which follow during this rural scene at the shepherd's cottage, the frank simplicity of Perdita in expressing her love for Florizel (his name itself being associated with flowers) communicates the rare quality of her nature. She typifies an attitude to life which is able to awaken in others a sustaining atmosphere of feeling, an inner support of law which, combined with love, is freedom.

This is what has been lost (Perdita) in our civilization, and it is what Shakespeare sought to restore by returning to the ageless vision of man and nature transmitted through the sacred inner realities of art symbolism for man's renewal of being. By means of Eleusinian mythology and the creative energy it channeled into the world, Shakespeare was clearly declaring his intention to restore the lost life of cosmic-spiritual meaning to art and, through this, to Europe. His emphasis on the feminine roles in this play seems designed to re-awaken living perceptions as distinct from, and beyond, the abstract ideas, scholasticism and rigid church dogmatism of his time.

A statement by S. Radhakrishnan summing up Tagore's philosophy of art covers our theme:

> Art is concerned neither with the actual and the imperfect, nor with the ideal and the hazy (i. e. the abstract), but the ideal immanent in it.
>
> *The Philosophy of Rabindranath Tagore**

---

* Macmillan & Co., London, 1919.

In other words, we are dealing with a functional merging of these two poles of truth. Everything hangs on our recognizing the organic principle of immanence as opposed to our modern exclusion of it. The prime issue, the rock on which civilization splits and is in danger of foundering, is the denial of this transfiguring immanence; namely, the presence and process of universal consciousness coming to self-awareness and identity in man.

We are close, here, to the meaning in Florizel's tribute to the spirit of joyous creativity in Perdita as a released power of transformation, a kind of activity which carries wholeness and divinity with it. (The word *divine* is of Sanskrit origin and means self-shining.)

> What you do
> Still betters what is done. When you speak, sweet,
> I'd have you do it ever; when you sing
> I'd have you buy and sell so, so give alms,
> Pray so; and, for the ordering of your affairs,
> To sing them too. When you do dance, I wish you
> A wave o' the sea, that you might ever do
> Nothing but that; move still, still so,
> And own no other function; each your doing.
> So singular in each particular,
> Crowns what you are doing in the present deed,
> That all your acts are queens.
>
>   Act IV, Sc. iv, lines 135-146

Such is the singularity, the unique yet utterly natural charm in the girl he loves which enraptures Florizel. Immediately following this speech, Perdita playfully calls Florizel by his assumed name, "my Doricles." The reason for the use of this classical name may be inferred from the classical myth-core of the play as a whole. In keeping also with the quality of wholeness which Perdita personifies, we have the following exchange between Polixenes and the shepherd on the subject of a dance they are witnessing. The former, referring to Perdita, observes:

> Nothing she does or seems
> But smacks of something greater than herself . . .
>
>   Act IV, Sc. IV, lines 157-158

And again, "She dances featly." The shepherd's reply to this last at once enormously widens and deepens the implication:

> So does she anything; though I report it,
> That should be silent; if young Doricles
> Do light upon her, she shall bring him that
> Which he not dreams of.
>
> Act IV, Sc. iv, lines 177-180

What is this if not a graphic way of suggesting the hidden source of all greatness, that of the expansive, life-giving power of spirit whether in nature, in man, or in his art: the power of permeating all actualities and particulars with itself for the birth and fruition of unfathomable meaning?

The essential likeness and harmony of the universe with man, and of man with the universe, is the eternal theme of our cultural system considered as a whole and at its highest. The realization of this fact places the finding of Perdita and the restoring of Hermione to life in their rightful symbolic position.

The great art of arts in which all the knowledge available to us in science, philosophy or religion ultimately unites, is that of right action, a combined spiritual and physical geometry in the use of our powers: the doing of all things as from a center from which they are seen as one. This is the vision out of which the Shakespeare plays were born. It can heal all conflicts because it harmonizes all opposites, including the relation of the sexes. It is for these combined reasons that the difficult role of the heroine is to be honored as that of an influence without which no transfiguring light of reality can fully dawn on our extremist world.

This lost art (Perdita) of life's renewal and totality — the forgotten recognition of the intuitively natural role of woman in the human scheme moves with grace and power like "a wave of ocean" through play after play, lifting and bending the often jagged lines of masculine force into curves harmonious with the universe.

The mandates of the heart rise like flowers from a common ground. They are unforced, but are the more com-

pelling for that reason. In Shakespeare the ruling influence
which prevails by its own inherent lawfulness and beauty
is an all-embracing and unconditional love for mankind.
Once felt, it rectifies the assumptions by which we ration-
alize our systems of exploitation and violence, until we begin
to sense within us the poles of truth on which the ultimates
of our destiny turn.

The Feminine Principle

In large part it is because of their depiction of woman
that the plays stand today so persuasively on the side of a
world revolution of human vision. The crux of our dilemma in this age of material force is summed up by Brutus
at the beginning of the second Act of *Julius Caesar*:

> The abuse of greatness is when it disjoins
> Remorse from power.
>
> Act II, Sc. i, lines 18-19

In this context the word "remorse" means compassion.
The statement goes to the heart of Brutus' problem in
motivation, or the relation of means to ends. Yet the sad
irony of such an utterance, coming as it does at this early
untested stage of Brutus' career, could not be more vividly
underlined than it is later on by the fact that his noble wife
and inspirer, Portia, commits suicide over his concealment
from her of his political designs.

In mentioning her death to Cassius, Brutus attributes her
act to impatience over his absence, together with fear of
the rising power of Octavius and Mark Antony. These
statements are utterly at variance with the fact that she,
as his wife, his "half," had pleaded to be allowed to share
in what was secretly tormenting him: the moral issue in the
plot to assassinate Caesar. His brief description of the manner of her death, that of swallowing fire in a fit of distrac-
tion, only further indicates his incomprehension of the
actual cause, which lay in himself.

To him the loss of his wife is a mystery, a fact which proves
his ignorance of his own public betrayal of principle in
"disjoining" compassion from power, as if the end justified
the means. What Shakespeare is bringing home is the fact

that the tragedy of Rome was the extension of a tragedy in the heart of Brutus: that of sundering the tie between love and reason which to Portia was mateship, even life itself. Her death thus symbolizes the death of something in himself.

During the historical period of transition selected for the play the highly civilizing influence of the Roman matron which had prevailed in the days of the Republic was being superseded. This decline was the hidden inner factor in the tragedy of Julius Caesar, consisting in the reduction of woman to the status of a sacrificial victim of the masculine power structure. It was the theme of Sophocles' *Antigone* in a new form, since the lost meaning of woman was typified by the ignoring of Calpurnia and Portia by their husbands. Significantly, too, the play marks a turning point in Shakespeare's thought in the direction of closer, more challenging analyses of the human scene, typified by *Hamlet, Troilus and Cressida, Measure for Measure, Othello, Macbeth,* and *King Lear.*

From all that has preceded in this chapter the role of the heroines, whether positive as in most of the cases selected, or negative as illustrated by Portia in *Julius Caesar* and by the pathos of Desdemona alluded to in Chapter I, it seems clear that Shakespeare intended to use this means of inaugurating a spiritual rebirth in the race mind. We have seen how the lost meaning of woman is linked in *The Winter's Tale* to the lost meaning of art, which, like "a wave o' the sea," carries with it an inexhaustible blend of nature, reason and love capable of lifting and bearing us along on the surge of its inherent force and beauty.

The comprehensive experience of the people and the world found in the plays is meant to provide a state of awareness, not an escape from ourselves. This new birth of life depends upon the reciprocal aid of man and woman through transcending their oppositeness in a manner which does no violence to the integrity of either. Rather does it enhance the One Life in each by an exalted interchange of polarities uniting them with the All. This is the entry into Shakespeare's realm of being which the present chapter has sought to explore.

The mythlike quality which characterizes much of the role played by the heroines is inevitable, owing to the hidden quality of the function they perform as modes of creative energy beneath our ordinary levels of awareness. In many instances they do improbable things or speak a forgotten language from depths we now ignore.

Few if any statements covering the whole area of this deep tradition can be found to match the suggestive power of the following sentences from the opening page of Joseph Campbell's *The Hero with a Thousand Faces*:*

> Throughout the inhabited world, in all times and under every circumstance, the myths of man have flourished; and they have been the living inspiration of whatever else may have appeared out of the activities of the human body and mind. It would not be too much to say that myth is the secret opening through which the inexhaustible energies of the cosmos pour into human cultural manifestation.

The key to the cosmic-human implications in Shakespeare is highly visible in the mythlike role of Perdita. Not only this, but a single phrase like "a wave o' the sea," suggesting the life-pulse of the universe, is descriptive of her spirit in action, revealing the significance which her enraptured lover saw in all that she was and did. It was applicable alike to her speech, her singing, her buying and selling, her praying, and the total ordering of her life.

Here the poet may be regarded as celebrating what the Greeks meant by the birth of Aphrodite from the sea: the feminine aspect of the creativity and beauty of the Holy Spirit which transcends all intellectual statements, but may be experienced as Reality through art. Shakespeare's aim was to restore the possibilities of this experience in renewed measure to our western civilization. Much the same emphasis on wisely directed feeling was later given lofty expression in Goethe's reference to "The Mothers" and to Helena in *Faust*.

Perhaps it is not extending this meaning too far to sug-

---

* Pantheon Books, Bollingen Series XVII, 1949.

gest that such heroines as Cordelia, Rosalind, Viola, Perdita and especially Portia in *The Merchant of Venice* are intended to awaken man to the role ordained for the feminine principle in each one of us and in the world process itself. The need of this balancing factor is now forced on us by the ugly drama of the streets where women are afraid to leave their homes at night. Similarly, perverse and sadistic arts born of abnormal sexuality, violence, cruelty and a general contempt for mankind are honored by magazines, movies, plays, novels and poems. There is a disturbing possibility in the prediction of a modern French poet that the nature of the 20th century may resemble that of the rake, Marquis de Sade. Stravinsky's opera "Rake's Progress" played at the Metropolitan in New York, is a case in point.

Wide adherence is given to the theory that art must be "outrageous," since the only positive assertion of freedom is held to be the unmotivated act, and the most convincingly unmotivated act is one of unprovoked cruelty. There is, nevertheless, ground for the expectation that current signs of a revival of moral philosophy, led by humanistic psychologists concerned with the alleviation of human pain, will suffice to redirect the current trend. This might invite a re-examination of the Shakespeare plays for exploring their still hidden insights into moral and psychic healing.

Chapter III

BE YOUR OWN HAMLET

We have been considering how the plays illuminate the spirit of woman in human affairs. We have seen this spirit in action as a needed factor in sensitizing, deepening and harmonizing the quality of our life. In the present chapter, as in those to follow, we shall feel our way into another area of wisdom and bring this likewise to bear on our work of self-knowing and integration.

The story of *Hamlet* is that of man's urge to mastery over his destiny. To be one's own Hamlet in the modern sense means, therefore, to awaken in oneself not only an urge but a commitment to follow a path of self-perfecting sufficient to surmount the downdrag and violence of our day.

As will be seen, Shakespeare's frame of reference includes the problem of heightening the state of knowledge and freedom existing throughout Europe. Limited as the situation in the play actually is, the scope of human awareness displayed by the hero contains the potentials of vision and fullness of life which our entire humanity now requires in its ascent toward freedom in diversity.

Unfortunately a preoccupation with Hamlet's "Oedipus complex" involving conflict between "resolution" and "thought" in his relation to his mother has tended to deflect modern attention from these far wider and deeper issues. In terms of history these are focused in the struggle for learning and enlightenment in Europe at the time of the Reformation, with the Danish court of Elsinore as a local setting.

At the same time, beneath this revolutionary effort we see Hamlet living through the profound allegory of his own self-awakening. With this focusing of history in the life of a single hero of vision, the hidden laws of universal being in man — the only ultimates of historical determinism — are raised into the mythic light of creative significance.

Within this psychological and historical frame of reference the play may be regarded as a key or test case for the entire study of Shakespeare. The Hamlet problem is actually the world problem and vice versa. It comes to a life-and-death issue in the self-awareness and action of a very human yet heroic individual. As an image of man at a time of great new stirrings in Europe, Hamlet gathers up in himself the crisis of his age and, on a still larger scale, that of our own.

The saying of Saint Exupery points up the function of drama in this respect: "If a man is to strive with all his heart, the significance of his striving must be unmistakable."

Prince Hamlet's problem and his commitment to it are presented in the opening scene by information received from the other side of death through the presence of the late King Hamlet appearing as a ghost. The rest of the play is to be understood as bearing simultaneously on the hero's outer and inner life, thus involving his knowledge of himself as a bridge between. In this way Shakespeare has provided a perspective for looking into the central problem of man: the linking of his separative mind-self or "earth" with what Hamlet senior represents symbolically as "heaven," namely the deathless father-self.

The ultimate precept given by the late king to his son, "Remember me," is taken by Hamlet with the utmost seriousness. He affirms:

> Remember thee!
> Ay, thou poor ghost, while memory holds a seat
> In this distracted globe. Remember thee!
> Yea, from the table of my memory
> I'll wipe away all trivial fond records,
> All saws of books, all forms, all pressures past,
> That youth and observation copies there;
> And thy commandment all alone shall live
> Within the book and volume of my brain
> Unmix'd with baser matter. Yes, yes, by heaven!
>   Act I, Sc. v, lines 95-104

In order to appreciate the full import of Shakespeare's

meaning, we need only to recall the revolutionary reversal in the direction of awareness and sense of value which marked the decisive moments of the main characters in several of the plays already discussed. These include: Romeo's "Turn back, dull earth, and find thy center out," Bassanio's acceptance of the challenge of the lead casket, Hero's willingness to "die to live" in *Much Ado About Nothing,* and Lear's final discovery of the fullness of the "Nothing" meant by Cordelia, a realization made possible by his own reduction to simplicity of heart.

Such instances of Shakespeare's recognition of "death" as the gateway to life point up man's destined realignment of consciousness, a law of adjustment familiar to us in the return of the prodigal son to his Father or in Plato's allegory of shadow figures in the cave. It is this which the poet introduces as his allegorical theme in *Hamlet.* It is the Prince's path of ascent to the perfection of his qualities.

The priority which young Hamlet gives to the remembrance of his father is emphasized by the secrecy he enjoins on his companions of the watch. This warning is repeated four times at his father's insistence. Furthermore the king's urgent manner alerts one to another of the author's purposes in the king's account of his death by murder while asleep in his orchard. The motive of the murder by Claudius, his brother, is unmistakable; but the method, that of pouring poison in his ears, is so unusual and subtle that it lends itself to far-reaching implications.

For Shakespeare, as for Bacon, attention given exclusively to materialistic learning and aims deadens the mind to the perception of higher realities. In this sense it is a kind of murder.

As for Prince Hamlet, it is evident from his filial dedication that something far deeper than ordinary affection or loyalty is involved. It is his affirmation of identity with a life principle at the center of his being. This response gains significance from the fact that beyond the general word "revenge," the late king gives no counselling as to affairs of state. In turn we may note that Hamlet's subsequent actions in setting right what is "out of joint," even when he is accomplishing his mission of revenge in ridding Denmark of Claudius, are all conducted in a spirit devoid of personal vindictiveness.

To be one's own Hamlet in the sense here suggested is thus to embark upon an expedition into oneself in a manner as simple and direct as it is profound. Shakespeare's implication would seem to be that such a procedure is relevant to the crisis of knowledge and the use of force which mankind now faces. Our failure to measure ourselves and our world against the deeper realities of life which underlie this play is an open confession of our lack of understanding of what is still inwardly required for achieving an integrated culture.

The pouring of poison in King Hamlet's ear acquires meaning when we connect its symbolism to the tyranny of the material mind which afflicted Europe and became a major issue for men of the Hamlet type during the Renaissance and the Reformation. Today the problem is still more evident when men in the position to make great decisions ask, "Who is man?" Only a balancing vision acquired from within at the point where the center-seeking and outward moving energies of consciousness meet can give us the required answer. These are Bacon's poles of truth.

We may now examine the play from three related angles: the political-religious, the broadly cultural and scientific, and that of the esoteric wisdom tradition. The convergence of these three lend historical significance to the play. Proceeding in that order, we see that the crisis produced at Elsinore by King Hamlet's murder immediately sets in motion political and military shock waves which run through the entire action until the cause is removed at the end with the death of Claudius. Orderly rule is reinstated by the accession to the throne of Fortinbras, Prince of Norway, after the death of Prince Hamlet. The effort of Claudius to eliminate Hamlet either by exile, murder in England, or finally, by poisoning through sword play constitutes the outer structure of the play. The pattern is typically simple and obvious.

A less obvious feature appears at the cultural level. For centuries the poison of blind faith, twisted doctrine and ignorance of nature had been poured into the ears of men until the future peace and destiny of Europe depended on the dethronement of this system. Indeed, the inevitable swing of the pendulum from blind faith toward what is now our modern materialistic skepticism was already gathering momentum. It was owing to these factors that the resulting rise of intrigue in Europe between the beginnings of the seventeenth and the nineteenth centuries became a menace which reformers such as Thomas More, Raleigh, Bacon and others clearly saw and attempted to mitigate.

In any case it is against such a background that we can most fully grasp the controversial problem of the meaning of *Hamlet.* When we place together certain references in the play, seemingly incidental but all pointing to the conflict that was going on, the present inference seems inevitable.

The appearance of the ghost of King Hamlet in the opening scenes of the play is accompanied by several striking allusions to the crowing of the cock. In the course of twenty-seven lines the bird is specifically mentioned five times, with emphasis on its function of awakening or bringing the day. This is far more than is required to indicate the generally accepted time for the retiring of a ghost. The implication of further meaning reaches its climax with Marcellus' pointed reference to a saying that at the season

> Wherein our Saviour's birth is celebrated,
> The bird of dawning singeth all night long.
>   Act I, Sc. i, lines 159-160

Hidden deep in this sacred context is an atmosphere of profoundest import, a note of expectancy, the full significance of which is lost unless we recognize in the crowing of "the bird of dawning" the Renaissance symbol for the awakening of freedom. This symbol was used by the troubadours in their songs and by the persecuted Albigensians and Waldensians in the form of water marks in their papermaking.*

In other words, the play opens on a revolutionary note which serves to alert us to other evidences pointing in the same direction in the course of the developing action. In

---

* See *A New Light on the Renaissance* by Harold Bayley, Benjamin Blom, Inc., New York.

the very next scene four references to Wittenberg, the place to which Hamlet plans to return for his schooling, link the meaning unmistakably to Reformation history.

The allusion to "windlasses" and "assays of bias" in the second act, dealing with the motivation of Polonius, suggests the inquisitorial spirit of medievalism.

Another major issue is introduced cryptically in the second scene by four lines of poetry written by Hamlet in a love letter to Ophelia. Polonius reads this uncomprehendingly to the queen:

> Doubt that the stars are fire;
> Doubt that the sun doth move;
> Doubt truth to be a liar;
> But never doubt I love.
> Act II, Sc. ii, lines 116-119

It is most extraordinary that Hamlet should couch a supposedly romantic note to Ophelia in terms so crammed with revolutionary dynamite! Here in four lines is the world-shaking challenge of Copernicus, Galileo and Bruno to the religious authority of the church which confined the scheme of human salvation and destiny to a tiny but self-sufficient corner of the universe, of which our earth was supposedly the fixed center with the sun and all else revolving around it.

Equally extraordinary is the view expressed by a noted modern scientist, who, in a radio commentary on Shakespeare broadcast by the British Broadcasting Corporation, stated that the poet was far too provincial, old-fashioned, comparatively backward and uneducated a writer to be cognizant of the new science which was changing the whole conception of the cosmic scheme. In support of his claim he cited the "terribly superstitous" reference in Shakespeare to ghosts, witches, and the influence of eclipses on human affairs. In other words he shuts the door on any supposition that the plays have the least scientific or practical relevance to the vast cultural issues of the time. For him Shakespeare was a provincial too removed from current intellectual stirrings to be considered seriously in such connections.

Shakespeare as a man of learning was fully aware of what

was going on in the world. The author of *Hamlet* knew what he was doing when, later in the second scene, he has the prince enter reading a book. Polonius in an ensuing conversation is baffled when Hamlet calls him a "fishmonger," a term which suggests the lucrative practice of the church in selling indulgences. Hamlet goes on to deplore the absence of honesty in the world and implies the need of new enlightenment in his reference to the sun's breeding maggots in a dead dog, as if a god were kissing carrion in the form of a decayed institution.

In similar vein Hamlet next refers to Ophelia by asking Polonius if he has a daughter, and on receiving an affirmative answer advises him ironically not to let her "walk i' the sun," an expression identifying her figuratively with the church, since the latter could not endure direct light and might conceive of things in an unorthodox manner. Hamlet's bantering advice to Polonius is that if he could walk backward like a crab, thus reversing his false direction, he would be as "old" — meaning as wise — as Hamlet. Polonius in turn begins to suspect that there is method in Hamlet's madness.

A few lines later (Act II, Sc. ii, lines 181-205) Hamlet epitomizes the whole situation in Europe when he refers to Denmark as "a prison." He extends the description to include the world in general "in which there are many confines, wards, and dungeons, Denmark being one of the worst."

For us this means that since civilization had been moving in the direction of blind credulity, thus prefiguring our modern opposite swing toward materialism, it was necessary to check the trend with something far nearer to blending man's faculties of thought and feeling in a manner capable of leading him toward peace. In place of a largely mechanical success motive such as now prevails, the energizing principle would have to be that of discovering one's own infinitude and the joy of unity within oneself and his fellows. This was the Hamlet task in the cultural revolution under discussion, just as it is still the mission of the Shakespeare plays as a whole.

When Rosencrantz suggests that Hamlet's sense of im-

prisonment is due to his ambition for power, Hamlet coun-
ters with the light of pure consciousness itself as its ascendancy over the relativity of conditions:

> O God, I could be bounded in a nutshell
> And count myself a king of infinite space.
> Act II, Sc. ii, lines 250-251

Admittedly he is oppressed by "bad dreams," meaning
the intrigues which he knows are set to trap him and are
opposing his efforts as a liberator.

At the close of Act II Hamlet has devised a plan for in-
serting a play within the play in order to expose Claudius'
guilt through his reaction to a scene depicting his murder
of King Hamlet. The device accomplishes a double purpose. It removes all lingering doubts in Hamlet's mind as
to the truth of the information given him by his father's
ghost. At the same time, but with far more urgency, it drives
home the meaning of the act of poisoning, the symbolic
import of which the ghost's brief original statement had
not fully communicated.

It is significant that this inner play occurs in the exact
middle of the enveloping one. The moment of crisis arrives when the poisoner advances to the sleeping king and
pours the fatal drops in his ears. This immediately produces its intended effect. Claudius rises and breaks away
from the assembled company, at the same time calling for
"light"! The word is picked up and emphasized by the
other members before the scene closes, leaving Hamlet and
his faithful alter ego, Horatio, alone. Could any other single word have been more expressive of all that Hamlet knew
was needed for setting to rights a continent as well as a
kingdom so out of joint?

The turning point of the play has been reached. From
here on the fate of Claudius is decided. His eventual death
at the hands of Hamlet is the physical settlement of the
political issue, but the end in view and the means are in-
extricably bound up with the cultural and psychological
issue.

What indeed if not light is the hinge on which the play
and the fate of the world turn? Since, as Carlyle put it in his

Heroes and Hero Worship, "The degree of vision that dwells in a man is a correct measure of a man," we touch here the supreme merit of Shakespearean drama in presenting life with a range and depth of movement capable of renewing vision and leading it toward total reality.

Ophelia's helplessness during the scene of drowning at the end of Act IV seems designed to suggest more than the feeling of pathos which the queen's poetical description creates. Once again there is a veiled identification of the daughter of Polonius with the institution of doctrinal authority. Although her father is now dead, she, upon falling into the brook, symbolizing the stream of time and history, is described as capable of self-help, and in her remaining moments she chants "snatches of old tunes" so long as her outspread clothing keeps her afloat. One senses in this the passing of an age which clings to old modes of thought, since it has lost contact with the spiritual energy of renewal required by advancing knowledge.

The swiftness of the fateful action in the closing scenes of the play brings into the sharpest focus the entire issue of justice, or moral cause and effect, which the two Hamlets, father and son, had referred to broadly as revenge. The Queen drinks the poison meant for Hamlet, and dies with a warning on her lips. Laertes, aware too late of the King's treachery, utters the words, "He is justly served" as, at a thrust from Hamlet's swordpoint, the murdering King is dispatched unrepenting to his death.

As Hamlet is dying, a flourish of drums and color announces the arrival of Fortinbras. The new regime takes control with promise of a happier future.

This concludes the present discussion of the play at its second level, that of the cultural issue which embraces so wide a field of human struggle. The stage is now set for examining at the third level the still deeper implications of what transpires in the ascent of Hamlet to a climax of spiritual attainment in himself. The story is wholly in the form of esoteric allegory. For the gist of it, the writer is indebted to a chapter in Claude Bragdon's *Old Lamps for New.**

---

* Alfred A. Knopf, New York, 1925.

In Prince Hamlet's relation to his father, we enter the dimension of man's dawning awareness of the causeless Cause or Source within him, of which the whole of his mortal nature is but the seemingly independent or separated expression. King Hamlet first gains our attention as a good but mortal man, now out of the flesh, who is bent on rectifying affairs at Elsinore through the agency of his son. For the latter, however, the commitment he undertakes assumes the aspect of an absolute responsibility amounting to loyalty to his own Higher Self, combined with an awareness of his very human conditioning by the circumstances of his environment.

The seriousness with which the prince at once responds to the beckoning of the ghost to speak with him in private prepares us for the profound intimacy of everything which follows. Despite Horatio's warning against a direct encounter, Hamlet follows the ghost "to more removed ground" declaring:

> What should be the fear?
> I do not set my life at a pin's fee;
> And for my soul, what can it do to that,
> Being a thing immortal as itself?
>
> Act I, Sc. v, lines 64-67

Such freedom from all ordinary self-concern indicates Hamlet's high qualification for receiving the solemn message imparted to him. The moment of communication with the spirit of his father is not to be regarded as merely a sensational or transphysical phenomenon, since the degree of his dedication is of supreme importance. His remark "I do not set my life at a pin's fee" conveys the key test of his condition. It is identical in meaning with the expression "die to live" or with other negations of the separate self already noted in the discussion of other plays. It is this which makes all higher fulfillment for man possible, since it opens the way for his realization of something beyond his ordinary egohood, namely his own divinity.

Hamlet has taken the first great step, one within himself, for his ascent to a life which transcends our mortal attitudes and limitations. From here on his many difficulties are not

final or decisive but only shadowy affairs he must deal with
on his way to ultimate victory.

Hamlet rises to the tremendous import of his dedication
in the lines already quoted, when the ghost says "Remember
me." Hamlet's reiteration of the phrase "Remember thee,"
with the concluding affirmation, "Yes, yes, by heaven"!
seals his total commitment, the word "heaven" being Shakespeare's term for the eternal principle in man. To say that
for him everything now hangs on his continuous thought
of his father is to state an unmistakable parallel to the spiritual self-commitment of man as set forth in Christ's admonition to his followers: "Do this in remembrance of me."

All of this serves to underline the real meaning of the
famous dictum from the lips of Polonius:

> To thine own self be true
> And it must follow as the night the day
> Thou canst not then be false to any man.
> > Act I, Sc. iii, lines 78-81

This is a priceless maxim to which Polonius was false. Were
this actually understood and lived, men would know their
true interests are harmonious throughout the world.

Here, through dramatic contrast in the play, is revealed
what Lord Bacon meant by "the discipline of the Ancients"
as the element in drama required to lead men to virtue.
Self-knowledge in the Hamlet sense is nothing less than the
supreme test of value of all other knowledge and experience. With this wisdom at the heart of Hamlet's dedication
to his "Father-in-heaven," we have the pivotal relation of
the play to the one Self in all men, that is, not to ordinary
maneuverings of the mind or to emotions as such, but to
the absolute fact of consciousness itself. In Hamlet's commitment, as also in the true but hypocritical words of Polonius on being true to oneself, we can discern the unitary
principle in man which is the origin of human justice and
well-being.

From this point on, the ordeal of Hamlet consists in confronting himself and the affairs of state in the light of this
new awareness. His trials and testings are encounters with
individual characters who personify lower aspects or false

identifications existing in his own nature. He is dealing
with the terrible errors and cruelties which arise from making decisions on the basis of man-betraying assumptions
about life or oneself. Thus his task of cleansing the court
of Elsinore and helping to bring freedom and order to a
world "out of joint" begins with faithfulness to the Reality
he has perceived within himself. It is in this sense that
Hamlet becomes his own myth-maker, a prince of being,
and by example points the way for man.

A little past the middle of the play Hamlet required a
reappearance of the ghost to "whet" his "almost blunted
purpose." The look of "piteous" appeal the ghost gave,
reminding him of the mission he had been delaying, became
a spur to further action.

The issue at stake comes to its inevitable climax in the
final scene. Hamlet confides to Horatio how some premonition had kept him from sleeping while on board the ship
to England and how, by secretly unsealing the packet the
king had given to Rosencrantz and Guildenstern for delivery
at the English court, he discovered his uncle's intention to
have him beheaded on arrival there. He explains that he
rewrote the commission, substituting the names of the two
agents for his own, thus bringing about their death.

In a series of self-questionings inspired by conscience he
makes the famous statement:

> There's a divinity that shapes our ends,
> Rough-hew them how we will.
>
> Act V, Sc. ii, lines 10-11

He justifies his action with the remark:

> 'Tis dangerous when the baser nature comes
> Between the pass and fell incensed points
> Of mighty opposites.
>
> Act V, Sc. ii, lines 60-62

He has already expressed his belief that the fates were with
him in the phrase:

> Our indiscretion sometimes serves us well
> When our dear plots do pall . . .
>
> Act V, Sc. ii, lines 8-9

This indicates that the discovery of treachery had renewed his failing determination to avenge his father's death.

The decisive factor is bound up with Hamlet's original motivation, namely his task of dealing with the intentions which determine action. In other words, the moral issue reaches beyond merely a question of Hamlet's saving his own life at the expense of the two agents of intrigue.

Still another question of conscience, the central issue of all, follows upon this. Hamlet asks Horatio if it is not a matter of "perfect conscience" as well as justice for him to kill the king, since it would amount to a crime for him to allow further evil to befall the state by permitting the king to live.

In this manner Hamlet finally resolves the problem which has troubled him throughout: the question of conscience as a scruple too often or too easily associated with cowardice. An additional premonition of personal ill, this time specifically connected with Hamlet's prearranged duel with Laertes, sets the stage for Hamlet's determination to proceed with his mission at all costs. It is this which leads to the death-transcending outcome.

By means of dramatic contrast the poet emphasizes the elements of mystery and meaning which surround the death of Hamlet and flow back into the play. In distinction from the other deaths, that of Hamlet is not treated as a mere ending. Instead it is a great transition. At this moment of hushed intimation we pass with him through the gateway of death into a beyond, an exalted heaven world suggested by Hamlet's simple but sublime expression, "The rest is silence."

Horatio links this death with a new and liberated life as he softly utters his closing

> Goodnight, sweet prince;
> And flights of angels sing thee to thy rest.
> Act V, Sc. ii, lines 369-370

At this moment we are close to a realm of consciousness where the God-mystery in man reveals itself in its own eternal silence. The parting is not a farewell, but a linking of earth and heaven. We are left with the feeling that Hamlet is now fully at home in a life that was beyond death from the beginning.

We may recall his early cry of longing, so reminiscent of the alchemists, when he first felt the weight of his spiritual task:

> O that this too, too solid flesh would melt,
> Thaw, and resolve itself into a dew!
>
> Act I, Sc. ii, lines 129-130

From then on, Hamlet's whole life was this process of "melting." Relevant to this we may note a statement in *Light on the Path* by Mabel Collins, regarding the ordeal to be endured by the man who would "enter upon the path of power." It is the work of conquering ambition, of tearing "the source of evil" out of his own heart until his whole life "seems to be utterly dissolved."

As we continue to reflect on Hamlet's career our understanding may widen. There may dawn on us the "wild surmise" that the play is an allegory of the poet's own life, symbolic of the ageless pathway he himself was treading as he progressively "died" to his separated selfhood and lived in a more total life-awareness. This inference may be drawn from the autobiographical character of his 146th Sonnet, ending with the lines:

> Buy terms divine in selling hours of dross;
> Within be fed, without be rich no more:
> So shalt thou feed on Death that feeds on men
> And death once dead, there's no more dying then.

This is the "die to live" motif the poet introduced lightly yet with psychological truth in *Much Ado About Nothing*.

Applied to Hamlet as a wisdom hero, the meaning of his death is a victory attended by flights of angels after he had slain the Claudius within himself. He has succeeded in the supreme human task of removing the personal self which separates man's consciousness from the oneness of all life and has opened direct awareness of his identity with universal being. He has slain the "Slayer of the Real"*

---

* *The Voice of the Silence,* by H. P. Blavatsky, The Theosophical Publishing House, Wheaton, Illinois.

within himself and is in direct contact with his Source. He has escaped from his own prison and is free.

Through the magic of art, Shakespeare is summoning us by life's own mysteries to surrender to the spiritual principle within us. With profoundly moving imagery he has spelled out for us what it means to be universal man.

Chapter IV

FROM *A MIDSUMMER NIGHT'S DREAM* TO *THE TEMPEST*

A Midsummer Night's Dream

The inexhaustible scope and timeless meaning of the Shakespearean world view may perhaps be best illustrated by placing together the two plays here cited. They face each other at opposite ends of an enormous area of human experience within which man's relation to nature and to himself is unfolding. As we perceive the movement of this life in the plays and recognize it in ourselves, we shall be sensing the relation of the individual self to the Universal Self.

The illusory events in *A Midsummer Night's Dream* and the symbolic happenings in *The Tempest* may be viewed not merely as cosmic inventions or serious-seeming fantasies, but as ascending levels of being. This process is an extended meditation on man's unfolding knowledge of himself. As we observe this process we may, like Lear at the summit of his life, begin to "take upon's the mystery of things."

Broadly speaking, this may suggest a new type of project in cultural anthropology in which successive stages in the evolution of consciousness are viewed as far as possible *from the inside*. It was Victor Hugo who first noted the basic difference between the human predicaments in *A Midsummer Night's Dream* and the state of affairs in *The Tempest*. In the first instance it was man's enslavement to forces not understood, and in the second it was his eventual rise to the mastery of those forces. We may add that the eonic past

of animal-like man is at one end of the spectrum, where
Bottom's dream of identity as an ass may remind us of the
centaur as a classical myth-image of man emerging from
animality. At the other end is the Promethean promise of
a future godlike humanity typified by Prospero's superman-
hood.

Within the enormous span of these two plays the poet is
showing us explicitly what he meant by Isabel's lines in
Measure for Measure:

> . . . Man, proud man,
> Dress'd in a little brief authority, —
> Most ignorant of what he's most assured,
> His glassy essence — like an angry ape
> Plays such fantastic tricks before high heaven
> As make the angels weep . . .
> Act II, Sc. iii, lines 117-122

These are the pairs of opposites, the "poles of truth," on
and between which Shakespeare sees the drama of human
destiny turning, with individual man in the role of consciousness facing matter. We shall be following these lines
of symbolic implication laid down by Shakespeare for tracing his vast design.

It is important to remember that in the new age of sea-
faring the data of geographical exploration lent great im-
petus to a mind such as his. It was inevitable that physical
and cultural meanings should converge in prophetic syn-
theses. Three centuries later the imagery in Keats' sonnet
"On First Looking into Chapman's Homer" was but an echo
of this expansive stirring.

In removing his characters in *The Tempest* to an island,
Shakespeare provides an unspoiled locality favorable to a
new and less trammeled scheme of things. In a fresh setting
such as this, conditions would favor the growth of a spirit of
brotherly enlightenment and self-change among men. One
sees in this imaginary westward adventure a recurrence of
the theme of a regenerated humanity in More's *Utopia* and
in Bacon's *New Atlantis*. In this context it is also meaningful to note the emblem which appeared as a frontispiece in
the first edition of Bacon's *Advancement of Learning*. It

showed a sailing vessel passing into the open Atlantic beyond the Straits of Gibraltar, or the Pillars of Hercules, and bore as a caption the phrase *Plus Ultra,* meaning "beyond the farthest." Again the pairs of opposites or "poles of truth" blend with Shakespearean terms and conceptions.

The animating spirit was that of Columbus, but at a higher level than that of geographical discovery. The total promise, when all of these clues and associated ideas are added up, includes a vision of arts and sciences leading to a new cultural and political order in the world. The further implications of this theme will be discussed in the final chapter of this study.

In *The Tempest* a resort to the symbolism of a remote western island in the Atlantic is further justified. Throughout Europe in the Elizabethan era, as in the time of Dante, imaginative literature was the accepted vehicle of wisdom, since torture and death awaited the exponents of truth who shared their revolutionary insights unconcealed by devices of allegory. The words of Hamlet are here indicative when he remarked to Polonius that to walk out in the air was to step into one's grave. It was in this sense that the illumined liberators of thought looked upon the whole of Europe, not merely Denmark, as "a prison."

The utmost human need was then, as it still is, to break out of the death-drift produced by the mind's extremes in the form of blind faith or materialistic skepticism. Thus the recognition of "the principle which gives life" — the principle of being which lies in consciousness itself and leads to "the sympathy of all things" — remains the most challenging area of exploration in Shakespeare. The plan to juxtapose *A Midsummer Night's Dream* and *The Tempest* has been undertaken as a means of attaining maximum entry into all of these dimensions of the Shakespearean vision of man.

In this connection it is suggestive that in the 1623 Folio edition of the plays *The Tempest* appears first. To the present writer the inference is self-evident that if the poet had wished to select one of his plays to serve editorially as an introduction to his over-all view of man's nature and spiritual destiny, he could not have chosen better. The

epitome of his entire scheme is in *The Tempest*. The common assumption that the author had little or nothing to
do with this edition and that the reason for placing *The
Tempest* at the head of the list was because of its immediate
popularity has only a secondary inference, not proof to rec-
ommend it.

The parallelism between the woodland in which most
of the action in *A Midsummer Night's Dream* occurs and
Prospero's sea-girt island in *The Tempest* has a certain significance. In both cases we are observing human nature
under conditions of withdrawal from civilization. The customary human codes, the familiar determinants of people's
attitudes to one another, are subjected to tests originating in
a direct contact with physical and psychic factors hidden in
nature. In both plays the central mode of effecting self-
knowledge is the familiar back-to-nature move, involving new
and unexpected confrontations of man with his environment, his fellows and himself. Sooner or later his traditional assumptions begin to fall away and a capacity for direct
observation and response awakens in him as from a dream.

The situation is comparable to that in *Alice in Wonder-
land* where the problem of distinguishing reality from un-
reality is a matter of perspective, not of things or experiences themselves. It is in this manner that the mystery of
consciousness reveals itself to itself apart from conditioned
thinking. In thus approaching the two plays in close se-
quence, we shall be following the poet's overall intention
of making us more fully aware of our whole psychic process.

In both *A Midsummer Night's Dream* and *The Tempest,*
it is only after the subjective encounters of the characters
with nature and with themselves that they return to civilization enlightened by their experiences. The important
thing is what has happened to them — and to us — in the
interim. At some point along the way we may recognize
ourselves as analogously undergoing somewhat equivalent
experiences involving a similar need to establish harmony
between the everyday self and its universal source within
us. Precisely for this reason and in this sense the realm of
being in Shakespeare invites us to approach our own mystery

and the living of it as a form of yoga.

The symbolism of moonlight in *A Midsummer Night's Dream* is sustained during most of the action as an overruling psychological factor. Seven references to moonlight occur in the opening scene, and in the rest of the play the word "moon" appears twenty-eight times. The woodland to which the lovers escape adds its enchantment to the atmospheric influence, with a touch of something else derived originally from the early English association of the term *wood,* or *woods,* with madness.

In other words, the conditioning of man by moonlight is obviously that of being lost or bewildered in a mental and emotional labyrinth created by the illusions to which he is subject. The influence is heightened, in turn, by characters belonging to the mysterious fairy realm of nature. Together these influences reveal or represent, as Victor Hugo put it, "the action of the invisible world on man," whereas in *The Tempest* we have a reverse situation depicting "the action of man on the invisible world."

Shakespeare's handling of dreams, including their prophetic character as already discussed in previous chapters, is indirectly clarified by his forty-third sonnet:

> When most I wink, then do mine eyes best see,
> For all the day they view things unrespected;
> But when I sleep, in dreams they look on thee,
> And darkly bright, are bright in dark directed . . .
> All days are nights to see till I see thee,
> And nights bright days when dreams do show thee me.

This archetypal meaning anticipates much of our modern insight into dream psychology. At the same time it may, from another angle, be associated with the glamor or witchery of moonlight occurring in *A Midsummer Night's Dream.* In this connection we should not overlook the fact, known to tradition, that the reflection of sunlight by the moon is analogous to the action of man's mind, since it is only a partial, shadowy function or reflection of the radiance of man's still largely hidden but essential principle of consciousness. We may infer here what has been known to mystics in all ages: that man's life is dreamlike, shadowy, unsubstantial and unsatisfying so long as he relies for guidance solely on his material intellect.

In short, man's knowledge of himself is incomplete and his actions distort life to the extent that his objective and subjective faculties fail to merge in a total awareness. It was this lost art of open, universalized perception which Shakespeare sought to restore or advance for the corrective guidance of the world during any such era of division, bias, and specialized "isms" as the one in which we now so precariously wander. We limit our comprehension of primary reality to its intellectual components and then proceed to identify ourselves with these at our peril.

The two plays, taken together, comprise a miniature cross-section of the world process which is endlessly unfolding itself in man. In the case of *A Midsummer Night's Dream,* a serious pondering on the relation of the moon to the sun may lead to an analogous correlation between the two worlds of external and internal perception. The external becomes meaningful only through the presence of the internal. In other words, we may recognize that both worlds are rooted unitedly in the core of our being.

Thus the mystery of our Self-knowing proceeds for Shakespeare, as ultimately for all men, in terms of the gradual but ceaseless expansion of a mighty mirroring. It is a divine interplay between man as a microcosm and the macrocosm in which he lives.

It is in this over-all context that we may find more than ordinary social significance in the opening scene of *A Midsummer Night's Dream.* When the arbitrariness of Athenian civil law governing marriage is challenged by the escape of Lysander and Hermia, followed by Demetrius and Helena, to the forest environment beyond the city, the stage is set for the beginning of a social revolution. The "property" right of Egeus in dictating Hermia's marriage choice in favor of Demetrius is dissolved in Act IV, for when Theseus is convinced that the two pairs of lovers have happily settled their conflicts in accordance with the laws of the heart, he overrules Egeus and invites the lovers to join him and Hippolyta at the temple in Athens for a wedding ceremony. By this action he is providing a concrete answer to the charge made by Bottom, while wearing the ass's head, that "Reason and love keep little company together nowadays; the more the pity that some honest neighbors will not make them friends."

Bottom's wistful comment brings us to the center of meaning in the play, as also to the dilemma of twentieth century man. It is the pivotal issue around which the whole "dream" problem and its resolution turn. The question is, which is the dream: Bottom's delusion of animal identity, or mankind's hope of realizing brotherhood? We are here at the "bottom" of our crisis in depth.

Accustomed as we are to the role of wisdom which Shakespear assigned to his clowns, we must acknowledge that nowhere else does this subtle voicing emerge with such seeming casualness, yet with such compelling point and from a source so ludicrous. All absurdity aside, the ignoring of Bottom's bedrock truth today is leading us to a competition of nihilisms.

Here in the guise of humor is the exact mixture of illusion and revelation on which the play is built. We are summoned to break out of the hypnotic spell of our materialistic folly — the resort of Egeus to force, in the guise of "law and order" — for the settling of a problem which, as Lysander, Demetrius, Theseus, and Egeus discovered, can be solved only by a combination of love with reason. The reversal of the death threat, imposed by Athenian law as a penalty for a daughter's disobedience to her father's will, constitutes the social phase of the pivotal action of the play. Viewed in the context of the world struggle today, it points up the need for a reversal of our way of thinking. Our alternative to Shakespearean comedy is Armageddon.

This issue between law and order, on the one hand, and reason and love on the other, is one of the ultimates of human existence thus mirrored back to us. Such a meaning, however, is almost certain to be lost unless we see relevance in what we so often take to be merely a whimsical outbreak of the poet's wit.

Bottom's comment on the nonsense of his dilemma is evidence of what the poet is intending when, in the next scene, Helena appeals to Hermia to remember the oneness of life they had shared in their childhood:

> We, Hermia, like two artificial gods,
> Have with our needles created both one flower,
> Both on one sampler, sitting on one cushion,
> Both warbling of one song, both in one key,
> As if our hands, our sides, voices and minds,
> Had been incorporate. So we grew together,
> Like to a double cherry, seeming parted,
> But yet an union in partition;
> Two lovely berries moulded on one stem;
> So, with two seeming bodies, but one heart;
> Two of the first, like coats in heraldry,
> Due but to one and crown'd with one crest:
> And will you rend our ancient love asunder
> To join with men in scorning your poor friend?
>
> Act III, Sc. ii, lines 203-216

Here we may ask, which is the illusion — their strife or their oneness? Occurring near the exact middle of the play, Helena presents in exquisite imagery the general truth already stated abstractly by Bottom. In both instances we come to supreme examples of Shakespeare's power as a myth-maker for purposes of man's self-mirroring and revelation. The whole foolish but painfully human dilemma of the play is laid bare in these lines. We sense here a universal entirety which lies at the center of the relation between substance and shadow, spirit and matter, identity and process — the author's message for our age.

The illustration makes clear how the realm of being in the plays discloses itself to us through the medium of art for our experiencing the unitary order of the world scheme in its polarity. Through the device of "dream" we come face to face with timeless realities by means impossible to rational techniques. In terms of ancient and modern depth psychology this leads to an understanding of the rhythmic interdependence of universal factors in the actual being of each one of us. Taken in this sense, *A Midsummer Night's Dream* is preparatory to the world message of *The Tempest*; the vision of man viewed individually and collectively as "a union in partition."

From this midpoint in the play the action is directed to

an awakening from the dreamlike state which brought the characters into heightened conflict. A general reversal of psychic direction begins with Oberon's instruction to Puck to anoint Lysander's eyes with juice sacred to Diana. The mythological association connected with the herb suggests the purifying power of discrimination and dispassion which leads to the release of man's higher consciousness from bondage to his lower. The latter state has been brought about by Puck's error in anointing the wrong pair of eyes with love-juice from the pansy. The symbolism of the two juices implies the balance of opposites underlying all manifestation.

As Oberon effects the removal of illusion, first from Lysander and then from Bottom, he reassuringly remarks that when those two characters return to Athens the adventures of the night will seem to them nothing more than "the fierce vexation of a dream." By analogy it is equally reasonable to expect that after the horror of modern wars, man will awaken to the realization that his agony was the result of his dreamlike ignorance of his own true nature. The secret of a creative balance between freedom and order lies here.

Bottom's account of his dream has something beyond his or any one's capacity to expound. The fact that it was bottomless suggests a special purpose in making him a central character of the play. There is more than humor in his verbal twistings when alluding to his dream and declaring that it shall be called "Bottom's Dream."

The very playfulness of the poet in presenting Bottom's inability to explain his dream carries with it a hidden meaning. Something beyond the merely ridiculous is indicated when Bottom tells the duke that the dream will be known as "Bottom's Dream" *because* it is "bottomless" and that he will "sing" it at the end of the play. This is a hint that the situation contains a further dimension, one which widens to include a background far wider than the dreamlike quality of the anxieties and frustrations of the lovers at the hands of an unjust legal code. In fact, the whole complex of confusion seems designed to appear dreamlike and unreal as contrasted with a deeper, more inclusive reality.

The enigma revolves around the problem of man's identity and goes beyond our laughter. For many a person there may

be moments when his customary frame of reference suddenly drops away and is replaced by the fleeting sense of a shift
or expansion of consciousness. Thoreau described this as
a "bottomless skylight in my life." Wordsworth called such
experiences "fallings from us, vanishings."

This is not to imply that Bottom was aware of matters at
this high level, but that through him Shakespeare was in-
timating the actual presence in man's unconscious of a
dim or partial glimmering of his origin and destiny: dreamlike vestiges of a background which is animalistic in one
direction and godlike in the other. By way of substantiating
the shadowy clues of a normally hidden past, we may cite
the tradition of wearing animal masks at Hallowe'en. Two
passages from the Bible are also singularly relevant.

In the Book of Daniel the account of Nebuchadnezzar's
dream contains a description suggesting the hero's passage
through pre-human stages of experience: He "did eat grass
as oxen" and "his hairs were grown like eagle's feathers and
his nails like bird's claws." (Daniel 4:33)

The 139th Psalm ends with a statement of the mysterious
process of form-giving which unites the cosmic with the human world in a manner resembling Shakespeare's description
of the poetic function as that of linking heaven and earth:

> My substance was not hid from thee
> When I was made in secret,
> And curiously wrought in the lowest parts of the earth.
> Thine eyes did see my substance, yet being imperfect:
> And in thy book all my members were written,
> Which in continuance were fashioned,
> When as yet there was none of them.

The forty-first stanza of Walt Whitman's "Song of
Myself" contains a statement of his awareness of life's abysses
in himself which parallels the passage from the Psalm just
quoted.

> Rise after rise bow the phantoms behind me,
> Afar down I see the huge first Nothing, I know I was
>   even there;
> I waited unseen and always, and slept through the
>   lethargic mist,

> And took my time, and took no hurt from the fetid
>   carbon.
>
> My embryo has never been torpid, nothing could over-
>   lay it.
> For it the nebula cohered to an orb,
> The long slow strata piled to rest it on,
> Vast vegetables gave it sustenance,
> Monstrous sauroids transported it in their mouths and
>   deposited it with care,
> All forces have been steadily employ'd to complete and
>   delight me,
> Now on this spot I stand with my robust soul.

We may add here that in Shakespeare we find occasional intimations of this enormous span of life-unfoldment in man, stretching from what he referred to in *Measure for Measure* as the "angry ape" stage to that of "glassy essence," or an unobstructed awareness of life's eternal expansion of its self-identity in individuals by right of an undivided heart, or self-awareness. In the plays, as in the sources just quoted, we come upon vistas of the vast interplay forever going on between life and form in the countless details of the cosmic human scheme.

The very transformations of mood or inner state occurring momentarily in individual characters are often used by the poet to reveal hidden depths occurring through self-change. One instance is the wonderful expression of relief voiced by Demetrius when he realizes the full import of the solution of his emotional conflicts as promised by the duke:

> These things seem small and indistinguishable,
> Like far-off mountains turned into clouds.
>   Act V, Sc. i, lines 191-192

Such experiences may be universalized through inwardly liberating shifts in perspective, thanks to the presence of the lordly duke principle which is at all times latent within oneself. In a corresponding way there is no limit to the depth of meaning we may find in the plays as we open ourselves sufficiently to reach beyond our ordinary categories of experience or thought.

The dreamlike element in *A Midsummer Night's Dream* consists, as it does in human life, in the confusion and conflict arising from errors in our sense of identity. Here, as in Shakespeare's earliest plays, it assumes a comic aspect. Yet in the present play the remedial function is clearly set forth as the special mission of the poet, described by Theseus in the last act as a glancing "from heaven to earth" and "from earth to heaven," or the awakening and release of the energy of unitary vision through linking together the subjective and objective poles of consciousness. Thus head-learning and heart-wisdom require each other if man is to be wholly man. Failing a discovery of this unifying center of balance within himself, the human entity falls into fantastic errors of illusion, conflict and destructiveness.

As if to poke fun at the illusory character of the walls of misunderstanding with which we divide ourselves from ourselves and from the world, Shakespeare includes the farcical playlet, "Pyramus and Thisbe." The ineptitude of the players is part of the satire. The wall which separates the lovers is, in the perspective of universal man, as irrational and impermanent as the Chinese or Berlin walls.

Nor does the relevance stop with these historic symbols. Far simpler but no less crucial is the wall of psychic self-division which modern commercial man sets up in himself by equating his sense of identity with the thing he is selling. To the extent that he externalizes his awareness of what he is by identifying it with profit and loss in handling commodities or exploiting the market, he is blocking off his awareness of his essential being. Unconsciously he becomes his own wall by dividing himself for the sake of marketing his "image" and thus enslaving the true unconditioned life of the spirit that is in him. In politics the same practice is all too familiar.

Shakespeare is gently reminding us that in every such case man is but struggling with the limitations imposed by his self-ignorance. It is all a kind of *Midsummer Night's Dream,* a shadowy half-world state of affairs, of which the farcical "Pyramus and Thisbe" is but a final reduction to absurdity.

Bottom's concluding remark that "the wall is down that

parted their fathers" serves the double purpose of universalizing the import of the entire play and preparing us for
Theseus' friendly invitation to the guests to retire for the
night. The final lines of the play gracefully introduce the
restorative, peace-giving aspect of the fairy influence. The
audience is left with a sense that the poet himself is awakening in us our own latent power of imagination for recreating
our world. It is this theme which will be pursued in the
following discussion of *The Tempest*.

The Tempest

Since *A Midsummer Night's Dream* is among the author's
earlier plays, it is natural to expect an enlargement and
deepening of scope in the later plays, particularly in *The
Tempest*, which we are now to consider. In bringing these
two plays together, we may more readily grasp the meaning
of their relationship if we note a few broad similarities in
setting and human circumstances.

The progression of psychological events in *A Midsummer
Night's Dream* extends, with allowance for a change in
characters, action and setting, to the more deeply allegorized
happenings in *The Tempest*. In each case the removal of the
actors from a conventional human environment to one of
contact with elemental nature allows freedom for exploring
the inner processes of human transformation. In each of the
two plays man is seen in the process of awakening from limitations imposed by his ignorance of what he is. This trend
in the two plays is the same, but the levels are different.
In both cases the poet's intent is profoundly integrative.

Relevant here is Paul Tillich's statement, "The finite
world points beyond itself — is self-transcendent." Such
pointing, reflected and actualized in man as a recognized
law of his being is the central design in *The Tempest*.

In the plays, with *The Tempest* as their climax, we have
the poet's prophecy of future man universalizing himself
at a point where freedom and order meet. This is now the
issue between the world's slow move toward ordered freedom on one side and its catastrophic urge to human manipulation on the other.

In this context there is point in noting the contrast in the opening details of *The Tempest,* revealing the two manners of arrival at Prospero's mysterious island. The entire first scene is one of storm in which the rugged seamanship of the boatswain makes the completion of the voyage of the royalty-bearing ship possible, except for the illusion of break-up and disaster at the end.

This is followed in Scene ii by Prospero's careful account to Miranda of their expulsion from Milan and from his rightful dukedom by his brother who set them adrift on the open sea in "a rotten carcass of a boat" without sail or tackle.

The location and nature of the island is supplied first by Ariel's allusion to the Bermudas and later by seemingly casual references during the long conversation among the characters throughout the first scene of Act II. Here the vague reference to a locality in the western Atlantic is blended with mythology for purposes of symbolism. The classical tradition of the Garden of the Hesperides and its golden apples was widely current in Europe at the time. By subtle indirection the poet refers also to the Celtic legend of the Islands of the Blessed. Actually, the tradition of a Sacred Island is of enormous antiquity going back to Central Asia. The Celtic Avalon is not mentioned by name, but in mythological research the fact has been noted that Gonzalo's allusion to the greenness of the grass and Sebastian's remark that Gonzalo is likely to "carry this island home in his pocket and give it his son for an apple" supply us with the needed clue to the identification: *aval* meaning apple and *yn* meaning green, thus Avalon.

The impression the poet creates is that of an unspoiled locality favorable to a new and less trammeled scheme of things where, under Prospero's guidance, opportunity would be afforded for the growth of brotherly enlightenment. One may see in this westward adventure an imaginative recurrence of the theme of More's *Utopia* and a prophetic actualization of the regenerated humanity which Bacon dreamed of in his *New Atlantis.* Further implications of this theme will be discussed in the final chapter of the present study.

If we may judge from references in *Pericles* and *The Win-*

ter's Tale as well as *The Tempest,* Shakespeare included a much greater span of time and cultural area in his plays than the episodes of Greek and Roman history he dealt with in *Troilus and Cressida, Coriolanus, Julius Caesar* and *Antony and Cleopatra.* By inference it is clear that the poet-mystic was intimately cognizant of the transmission of wisdom lore in the eastern Mediterranean regions of Egypt, Phoenicia, Libya and Chaldea. His reference to Pericles as "Prince of Tyre" carries overtones when we recall the fact that Pythagoras was a Tyrenean. In *The Winter's Tale* Florizel, in his concocted story of Perdita's origin, presents her as from Libya and daughter of a king. The reference to Dido in *The Tempest* links our thought with Carthage, known in ancient times as Tunis. Theseus in *Midsummer Night's Dream* is Duke of Athens, that city of prehistoric origins traced back to Egyptian civilization, and with Eleusis, site of the mysteries, so much a part of its history.

The city of Ephesus, so often used in the plays, was renowned for its temples and a magnificent theater, as well as being an important Greek commercial center — a combination of interests which typifies the gradual transmission of thought westward from India through Persia to Asia Minor.

Etymologically this fact would seem to be borne out by the meaning of the name *Ephesus* itself, since the Greek root *pha* meaning *light,* (compare the Egyptian word Pharaoh) is derived from the verb *phao,* to shine, and this, according to linguists, seems certain to have come from the Sanskrit *bha,* a generic word for *being.* When we also take into account the prefix of Ephesus, the *e* in Greek meaning *from,* we have in the name of that city a remarkable profundity.

Applied to man, it signifies one who lives from or in the central light of his being, the immortal principle which illuminates the Shakespeare plays. It was from the safe island of oceanic consciousness within him that the poet projected his vision of Prospero as a prototype of man's eventual self-sovereignty and collective understanding.

This accounts for the mythlike Promethean quality in Prospero, oriented, as his name implies, to the future, "I hope forward." Indirectly the Promethean theme of Aeschy-

lus reappears in the hero of *The Tempest*. He is the image
of authentic man whose regenerating fire of enlightenment,
gained by an ordeal of self-transcendence in defiance of the
lordly Zeus, works with the magic of art to release mankind from enslavement to delusions. Prospero, like the
poet himself whose alter ego he is, lived to awaken in others
the capacity of vision and self-responsibility required for
the future dawning of a peaceful world.

Among these suggested meanings we should include that
of Prospero's daughter Miranda, a name indicating the act
of wonder and therefore Platonically linked to the birth of
wisdom.

We have been considering Shakespeare and his wisdom
hero, Prospero, in the light of the prophetic tradition. We
have now reached the point where the massive import of
The Tempest may be viewed and felt in its relation to the
humanistic crisis of the late sixteenth century in Europe
and likewise of our time. In both cases the question of the
kind of man the existing culture produces becomes a dramatic issue in itself.

One may readily infer Shakespeare's concern on this score
from evidences in *Cymbeline,* a play close to *The Tempest*
in date of composition. In it we find that the early English
integrity of character, together with physical vigor nourished
in a rugged environment remote from court life, proves
capable of withstanding the corrupting influences spreading
northward from Italy, then past the peak of its Renaissance
flowering.

In *Cymbeline* the author is obviously guarding the political and moral integrity of England. He is using poetical
drama to reawaken among his people their needed recollec-
tions of a heritage of character and mission which was in
danger of sinking into eclipse before the advancing shadow
of a materialistic and skeptical vision of man.

Beginning with the third scene of Act III in this play, we
find emphasis on soundness of character and tradition which,
in its relation to the nature setting provided for it, reminds
us of the poet's earlier and more fanciful handling of this
theme in *As You Like It, Twelfth Night,* and *A Midsummer
Night's Dream*. In *Cymbeline,* however, nature and imagina-

tion combine with history in a more direct and serious intent. Emphasis is given to the independence and sturdiness of the early English people in protecting themselves and their land from serfdom to Rome. This in turn assures a background for the moral climate the poet needed for presenting the queenly character of Imogen as a symbol of the true royalty and incorruptibility he desired for the guidance of his nation. It is in this context, too, that his historical plays as such may be sensed in all of their actuality and realism as revolving around the largely hidden center of ideal rulership.

The relation of all this to *The Tempest* can be seen when we consider the fusion of history, ethics and psychology in *Cymbeline* as an intended counterforce to the enfeebling licentiousness and casuistry of Italian thinking in the 16th century. The political aspect of that trend was powerfully set forth in Machiavelli's view of man as naturally brutish and requiring government by fear and force. To Shakespeare and the Platonic tradition of the philosopher-king this swing of the pendulum was as dangerous as the blind faith which had ravaged Europe with torture scarcely a century before.

Admittedly the predatory and sensual traits of man depicted in the lower characters of *The Tempest,* from the subhuman Caliban on up, call for stringent discipline. Even Ferdinand, the ideal object of Miranda's love, is not permitted to take things too much for granted. Nevertheless at no time does Prospero assume any of these characters to be incapable of guidance towards self-improvement. Without exception, stirrings of their own higher possibilities begin to occur during the experiences he arranges for them.

The result is that the entire process shines before us in its symbolism as an example of benevolent spiritual energy working creatively with the laws of nature for human redemption. There is no trace of cynicism, brutality or revenge in Prospero's conduct of affairs, despite his needed sternness in dealing with Caliban and a tendency to gruffness in his initial manner towards Ariel. Insofar as this latter trait is a failing, he amends it when Ariel gently proposes an attitude of mercy and tenderness toward the schemers who would wrong him.

It is hard to imagine a greater contrast than this to Machiavelli's idea of the state as a morally isolated entity in which human nature is treated with little regard for its improvement, least of all for its relation to something as poetical yet real as the cosmic harmony. Such a vision had no place in his scheme of practicality.

These general considerations lead to a closer look at Prospero's ordeal in accepting the loss of his dukedom. Undoubtedly his deep studies had prepared him for a philosophical acceptance of his humiliation. Nevertheless the path which he, like all such heroes, must travel involved a superrational adjustment, a "dying" to, or ceasing to be identified with, his mortal selfhood and its circumstances. In the face of all outer turns of fortune he must stand aside, firm in his awareness of the eternal principle within him, the presence of "Providence."

Two equivalent instances in the plays not previously cited may be mentioned here. One is the advice given by the duke to Claudio in the prison scene in *Measure For Measure*. When Claudio is asked if he hopes for pardon, he replies: "I have hoped to live and am prepared to die," whereupon the duke advises,

> Be absolute for death; either death or life
> Shall thereby be the sweeter.
> Act III, Sc. i, lines 4-5

A second example appears at a dramatic moment in the crucial fifth act of *Timon of Athens,* where Timon, renouncing war and leaving Athens to the fate she had brought on herself, speaks in a manner reminiscent of Job or Socrates:

> My long sickness
> Of health and living now begins to mend,
> And nothing brings me all things.
> Act V, Sc. i, lines 189-191

Such wisdom is too often regarded as a flight of the poet's whimsicality appearing in the characters. Nevertheless his serious intention is made evident by his consistency and by the ensuing consequences. The result is an awakening of wholeness. It is for these reasons of total harmony of being that the discovery and occupancy of Prospero's island represents the ageless quest of all mystics, the heart of the teaching of all sages.

Shakespeare's over-all theme in *The Tempest* points forward to the eventual victory of man as a conscious embodiment of the universal life, converting into sublime opportunities the very limitations, conflicts and defeats which he endures. Prospero's island is closely allied in meaning to Buddha's likening of man's inmost consciousness to an island to which he should resort for reflective self-awakening and ultimate mastery of existence. The island is the point of conjunction between man's particular and universal attributes of selfhood. It brings him and the cosmic order into a single focus. As such it is Shakespeare's inner heaven of creativity, the realm of the "magic of the soul," to use Goethe's description of art.

Once we grasp the full import of Shakespeare's blend of historical, philosophical, ethical, psychological and cosmic elements in his plays, we cannot avoid the conviction that in *The Tempest* he is in company with the supreme mythmakers of all time. In his island symbol the myth-function rises out of the sea of being and renders man cognizant of hitherto unrealized potentials of wisdom, freedom, and order within himself. Thus we are witnesses of those hidden breakthroughs and awakenings — visible in the other plays and here mounting to a climax — which render us capable of transcending adversity and transforming pain.

In view of the dividedness now existing in the world, it is self-evident that an attitude of life, conveyed by voyages to the wisdom within and a reaching beyond technology, is required in our cultural system if we would avoid destruction. It is significant that the theme of *The Tempest* was first illustrated in a contemporary frontispiece showing bright beacons in a harbor of safety during a storm. It is hard to surpass the relevance of this for man living in the hurricane of the twentieth century. Nor should we entirely close our minds to what may be implied by the fact that the English pronunciation of the *ea* in *beacon* was that of a (as in Bacon).

The remaining part of this chapter bears on Shakespeare's further use of incidents and symbolic devices as modes of transmitting the wisdom tradition for use in ages to come.

On a close examination of Prospero's manner of reacting to his loss of worldly status as duke of Milan, one is struck with his involved manner of speaking to his daughter Miranda, although twelve years had passed since his actual ousting, and the girl, who had been a small child at the time, was now in her middle teens. The account is placed in the second scene immediately following the storm scene with which the play opens. Thus the atmosphere of storm and extreme hazard is carried over with only a minimum break, and the full force of Prospero's ordeal of anxiety is felt as a test of faith and courage prior to the seeming miracle of his safe arrival at the island. The experience was one of utter extremity and involved literally all that was in the man.

In the opening portion of his story Prospero admits his responsibility for having neglected full attention to the official duties of his office in favor of private studies for improving his mind, with the result that he failed to detect his brother Sebastian's evil designs before it was too late. He explains that he had entrusted some of the affairs of state to his brother because he loved him, implying also that his own devotion to the liberal arts was in keeping with this as evidence of his over-all attitude to life. Thus it is clear that his loss of the dukedom was not due to lack of capacity, but to overconfidence in his brother's integrity, and that the loss had come as a double shock.

The next phase of the story, that of physical danger, comes when Miranda asks:

> What foul play had we that we came from thence?
> Or blessed was't we did?

Prospero's answer is a swift, emphatic summation of the crisis:

> Both, both, my girl:
> By foul play, as thou say'st, were we heav'd thence,
> But blessedly holp hither.

> Act I, Sc. ii, lines 59-63

These two statements lead to revelations of matters which are obviously of intense concern to Prospero and, seemingly, in their range of political reference and repeated emphasis of expression, to the poet-author himself. By inference we are brought face to face with an example of Shakespeare's own awareness of the fact that the colossal range of his knowledge, including his inside familiarity with European as well as English court life and history, could not be reconciled with the stock image of a poet or playwright of rural background. Such a phenomenon still strains the credibility connected with the Shakespeare tradition.

In any case the evident earnestness of Prospero's concern at this point in his narrative serves to alert us to the fact that he is wisely in command of himself and of events. In contrast to Miranda's recollection of the fated ship and its passengers, he assures her of their safety. As a token of his guiding wisdom in cooperation with "bountiful Fortune," he lays down and then resumes a magic mantle which he terms "my art."

From this point on there is no mistaking the symbolic role of Prospero as an exemplar of the mission of the ancient mysteries boldly made visible on the public stage. The exalted ethics he embodies and the influences he sets in motion in the lives of those around him, including his enemies, reveal him as a masterly exponent of the higher laws of the evolution of consciousness. Thus to be one's own Prospero and to find and occupy his island is the ageless goal of all mystics, the heart of the teaching of all sages.

It is important to grasp the significance of Prospero's words and manner in answering Miranda's indirect query as to how they had reached the island. In a few lines he reveals the crucial, agonizing ordeal of their sea experience in "the rotten carcass of a boat." For him all the potentials of his nature were gathered to a point in facing the immanence of total defeat and destruction. This was his ultimate test and struggle, the gateway of apparent death through which, as so often in Shakespeare, the hero or heroine must pass before attaining release into a consciousness far deeper and more vast.

The most striking yet condensed instance of this inner

struggle and reversal to be found in Shakespeare is the one so briefly alluded to by Prospero in his account of things to Miranda. She is torn by the thought of having been a care to him, but he emphatically reassures her of his gratitude for her childhood innocence and comforting smile while he shed "salty tears" on the waves. The very brevity of his description coupled with Prospero's single word "Providence" to account for their safe arrival at the island gives emphasis to what is said. We shall come near to the meaning of this word as used by Shakespeare in the wisdom tradition if we associate it with the God-principle in man himself.

The final necessity of this transition has been stated by Radhakrishnan: "So long as we feel ourselves to have individualities of our own, we will be beset with conflicts and contradictions." In Prospero's case the poet helps us to witness the making whole of a divided man.

In *Hamlet* the hero fully reaches this point only at the end of the play. In *The Tempest* we observe the continued career of the hero as he lives on, no longer critically embattled by his own qualities or by those of plotters against him — the attitudes and motives imposed by the material mind. This truth of the Prospero story has a meaningful bearing on the crisis in America.

It is significant that as a poet, psychologist and realist, Shakespeare is in company with the supreme myth-makers of all time when he presents Prospero's island as a point of awareness in man through which the universal life may pour without loss of its own infinitude. In this symbol the myth-function rises out of the sea of being and renders man cognizant of a hitherto unrealized source of wisdom within himself. Thus in Shakespeare we are witnesses of those hidden breakthroughs and awakenings which render us capable of transcending adversity and transforming pain.

We may gain a sense of realism concerning Prospero's sea experience from a modern narrative *Kontiki,* recounting the actual voyage of six men on a balsa raft from the coast of Peru to one of the Polynesian islands. After weeks of moving under sun and stars across the spaces of the Pacific, the pilot-author, Thor Heyerdahl, recounts his sense of the merging of time, space, and human affairs in a single point of significance within himself. This was symbolized for him by the little rustic cabin on the raft, which became a center of reference for the timeless security he had inwardly come to feel at special moments.

In *The Tempest* the long second scene of Act I continues after Miranda falls asleep. The movement is rapid and varied, first introducing us to Ariel and then to Caliban, together with their backgrounds and relations to Prospero. The range and quality of the latter's wisdom in dealing with these contrasting types prepares us for his practical balance of foresight, firmness and consideration in arranging matters equably, later on, for his human friends and enemies.

Atmospherically a linkage of the play to *A Midsummer Night's Dream* exists insofar as sorcery exercised by "the foul witch Sycorax" may remind us of the mishaps in the fairy world of Oberon and Puck. But there is no equivalent in *A Midsummer Night's Dream* to the subhuman dregs of motivation represented by Caliban.

The tone of *The Tempest* scene just referred to rises as Prospero commands Caliban's exit and Ariel reenters invisibly, but playing music and singing. Ferdinand, who has been grieving over the apparent loss of his father, the king, explains that he has followed the music as it "crept by" him "upon the waters."

At this point the "sweet air" takes form in words of the most exquisite symbolic description of Nature's process in the psychic transformation of man. For simple depth, range, compactness and beauty of expression and meaning it is unequaled in the English language:

> Full fathom five thy father lies;
>> Of his bones are coral made;
> Those are pearls that were his eyes;
>> Nothing of him that doth fade
> But doth suffer a sea-change
>> Into something rich and strange.
>>> Act I. Sc. ii, lines 396-401

As Ferdinand rightly observes,

> This is no mortal business, nor no sound
> That the earth owes.
>
> Act I, Sc. ii, lines 406-407

We are indeed in the realm of subtlest inner processes, and in his reference to "sea-change" the poet has given us a consummate image of the vast hidden work of his world vision and art. We sense the mode of this deepening of man's life-awareness and sense of identity by a natural exaltation of the intelligence — not by drugs!

One is reminded of Hamlet's longing to "melt" the fleshly limitations of his understanding." In *The Tempest* it is more obviously a case of "deep calling unto deep," the work of a sea-like immersion of consciousness in its own nature, thus knowing itself to be undividedly one and continuous with life, within and without. Lit with this illumination, the eyes of man may indeed become like jewels.

In the first scene of Act II there is bantering talk between several of the passengers including Gonzalo, the old counsellor, about the symbolism of the island. The latter is jocosely referred to as an apple (mentioned previously in our discussion), the seeds of which will be sown in the sea "to bring forth more islands", that is, to promote the wisdom tradition in Western culture. In the same droll yet intentional manner Shakespeare has Gonzalo broach the Utopian theme of an ideal commonwealth, all of which means nothing to Alonso.

The tone of this satire on human skepticism as to man's perfectibility quickly deepens into a life and death issue with the plot of Sebastian and Antonio to murder the now sleeping king. This is followed in Act III by Caliban's intent to ravish Miranda and, with the aid of Stephano and Trinculo, to dispose of Prospero and take over the island.

Thanks to Prospero's vigilance and Ariel's magic, these schemes of crass self-interest are frustrated. The references to the bellowing of bulls, the barking of dogs, and the apparition and disappearance of a feast constitute vestiges of procedures in ancient initiatory rites for testing the worthiness of candidates in facing the trials of life's dangers and illusions.

From the beginning of Act IV the play rises to a triumphant completion of the regenerative processes which Prospero had set in motion. A fuller meaning of Shakespeare's description of the role of the poet in linking heaven and earth, as described by Theseus in *A Midsummer Night's Dream,* appears in the invocation by Prospero of the goddesses Iris, Juno and Ceres to help, in the words of Iris, "to celebrate a contract of true love" between Ferdinand and Miranda. This is no mere decorative flourish of Greek religious pageantry, but a climax of symbolic patterning.

In the training of will and dedication which Prospero had given Ferdinand by making his physical labors arduous, and then in the intimately preparatory instructions he had also given the young man concerning the exalted character of the nuptial act, we are looking into the heart of Shakespeare's conception of nature, life and civilization as essentially one vast process of power and beauty, by invoking which the spirit of art can draw forth the enduring and ennobling elements in man as parts of a universal existence.

What had been in *A Midsummer Night's Dream* a rightful re-ordering of confused love relations is, in *The Tempest,* lifted to a transcendent level where the heavens open, disclosing the actuality of living forces which the Greeks personified as deities — in this case Juno and Ceres, preceded by Iris. In the context of this cosmic myth the role of Iris, goddess of the rainbow linking heaven and earth, is Shakespeare's most exquisite symbol of the light-bearing function of the poet. It reminds one not only of Bacon's description of ancient drama as "the musical bow of the mind," but still more of the meaning which one of Lao Tze's disciples had in mind when he was reported to have said, "Man is a prism through which the rainbow of the Great Existence is to shine."

Such is the sacramental background of love which the world's master poet has left us, using symbolism to place in true perspective the opening of life to a larger consciousness at the moment of great events, including not only marriage but, as in the other plays, man's arrival at birth, citizenship and death. Viewed in this light, Shakespeare's own art, like the apparent statue of Hermione in *The Winter's Tale,* comes to life as a human fulfillment of the deathless creative energy of Nature, the mother principle of life itself.

By contrast it is pertinent to observe that in an equivalent way the plays reveal how, with the disappearance of reverence for life, a spirit of violence fills the vacuum and causes men and nations to decline or disappear.

Some of the most striking and memorable lines in all of Shakespeare are those in which Prospero brings home to us the airy, dream-like unsubstantiality and impermanence of everything material we build on:

> Our revels now are ended. These our actors,
> As I foretold you, were all spirits and
> Are melted into air, into thin air;
> And, like the baseless fabric of this vision,
> The cloud-capp'd towers, the gorgeous palaces,
> The solemn temples, the great globe itself,
> Yea, all which it inherit, shall dissolve
> And, like this insubstantial pageant faded,
> Leave not a rack behind. We are such stuff
> As dreams are made on, and our little life
> Is rounded with a sleep.
>
> Act IV, Sc. i, lines 148-158

It took Einstein's discovery of the exact nature and full range of physical relativity to stir us to a partial acceptance of this fact. Yet Shakespeare goes farther in his cyclic implications respecting the cosmic scheme.

What can be our conclusion except that here science and poetry, or the wisdom tradition, meet? We stand on the shore — perhaps an island — of a sea of truth by no means yet fully perceived and far less lived. Sir James Jeans, in *The Mysterious Universe*, was actually reaching a point-event of convergence with Shakespeare when he noted that science has resolved our solid-seeming world into "a flow of waves."

By inference drawn from all three sources we are brought to the inescapable conclusion that the hard fixities we artificially impose on life and on each other by our identification with material conditionings, by our technologically enforced ideologies and by our conflicting power structures, are at bottom illusory and that a reversal in our thinking is a necessity if we are to enter knowingly into the stream of life and consciousness as such.

The happy conclusion of *The Tempest,* in which all enmities are forgiven and the characters return to their starting point for a resumption of life at a more enlightened level is proof that at last the interactive relations of all things within nature, human and otherwise, are beginning to be understood. It is all a dramatically projected study in what might be termed the wisdom of cosmic-human ecology. In aim, if not method, it has something in common with the working of human attitudes in relation to universal laws as livingly symbolized in the Chinese masterpiece, the *I Ching*.

The assumption is warranted that with this play the poet went far to imprint upon the mind of the race those "same footsteps of nature" to which Bacon alluded when he affirmed their presence throughout the universe. As with all true sages, Shakespeare consistently demonstrates that our awareness of these correspondences is the thing which matters in our affairs, and that the well-being of the world depends on the extent to which each individual finds this meeting of finite and infinite in himself.

In summation we may regard the story of Prospero as Shakespeare's most complete allegory of what transpires in man in the course of his ascent out of the unconscious to a more total awareness and mastery of his being. In full accord with mythological tradition, the way of ascent is depicted as leading through storms and across the waves of life's infinite diversity of conditions, eventuating in a unitary perception of the essence of things, a higher-dimensional capacity symbolized by Prospero's island center of consciousness. "If thine eye be single," we are told in Christian scripture, "thy whole body (i. e. existence) shall be filled with light." (Luke 11:34).

In one form or another the dynamics of this vision constitute the central shaping power at work in or behind the scenes in all of the plays, even, by reverse implication, in the darkest tragedies. To a poet-philosopher-seer man's very denial of his spiritual source and birthright is not an absolute phenomenon, but a relatively transient shadow-phase of the process of his growth, implying the presence of the very potentiality of godlike perfection in which he is rooted. It remained for Shakespeare to gather the rays of his own cosmic illumination into a single focus in *The Tempest* and reveal in one supreme art form the directing principle of the wholeness of being he had attained. Like other supreme masterpieces of world culture, the plays as a whole and *The Tempest* in particular are focused to a seeing of things objective in the light of the subjective, that is, as expressions of universal consciousness itself, the experience of which is forever new, unconditioned, liberating.

Chapter V

TROILUS AND CRESSIDA AND THE UNITED STATES: A SHAKESPEAREAN TRAGEDY?

Truth means the realization of our being.
The true relationships of things are harmonious.

The Trojans

The subject of voyaging dealt with in the preceding chapter will serve as a transition to this concluding one. All of the earlier chapters may, in fact, be regarded as preparatory to this, since the issues of life and death which are there correlated with the problem of freedom and order in the individual man now come to the surface in Shakespeare's most broadly compelling and socially decisive manner. The writer is confident that in such a perspective the study of the plays can no longer be regarded merely as an academic enterprise, but rather as a call to action.

The direction of certain rays of the Shakespearean vision of man will now be shifted from Europe and trained on the American scene as a major focal point of our world problem in its present critical phase. Up to this point the plays have been selected and viewed as a kind of galaxy shining above and around us, each play serving as a mirror to awaken in us some aspect of the wisdom man needs in his now most crucial task of self-knowing and liberation from the misery of his own conditioning.

Let us think of the United States as a vastly extended Shakespearean drama, with the width of a continent for its stage, and its original plan, like that of the plays, designed for the education of men in the reality of the united spirit of life. Historically and psychologically the time had come in the course of human events for a large scale experiment in man's capacity for individual and collective self-government.

Only at rare, brief intervals and in restricted areas has civilization attained a balance of freedom and order in human relations. In all other eras this has been the stumbling block. However, man's new command of the physical conditions of living has prepared the way, as Teilhard de Chardin has stated, for a transition in consciousness. Thus the global character of man's environment combines as a factor with the range and speed of his intercommunication to force his awareness of life to curve back on itself toward a central point of identity and total reference. The fact that this is occurring simultaneously with the outreach of human imagination into space must inevitably lead to new dimensions in man's awareness of consciousness itself and in his appraisal of where and how he stands in the total scheme of things.

The obvious need of this type of insight, coupled with Einstein's warning of catastrophe unless we change our ways of thinking, adds immeasurably to the timeliness of the ethical as well as the poetical art of Shakespeare. Our concern in this chapter is the bearing of these combined factors on man's self-discovery and transformation, particularly when related to the principles of citizenship incorporated in the American dream. The present meaning gains point when taken in context with the propositions and symbols on which this country was founded. The reasons for selecting *Troilus and Cressida* for our final discussion will be seen in the deep implications it has in theme and structure relative to the dichotomies of thinking which now so dangerously divide all unity of life in the United States. This applies to divisions in other countries also.

In examining this play we shall dismiss the widely accepted view that the poet's main intent was to satirize and deflate the legendary war heroes of Greek tradition. Other factors stand out so predominantly and are of such universal import that their meaning for our time calls for major attention.

Ostensibly the cause of the Graeco-Trojan war was the abduction of Helen, wife of the Greek King Menelaus, by Paris, son of Priam, the King of Troy. In turn the one condition for lifting the siege of Troy by the Greeks was the restoring of Helen. The issue was fatally complicated by the Trojans' continued rejection of this rightful demand after seven years of fighting. It is pertinent also to suggest that for Shakespeare the issue reached beyond the obviously partisan, patriotic, or even moral angles into depths of Homeric allegory congenial to the dramatist's conception of woman.

This implication gathers further point when the name of Troy as a city is associated with that of Troilus, a word which, when hyphenated as Tro-ilus, signifies an association of the community as well as the man with the meaning conveyed by *ilus*, the Greek word for mud. In other words, we are given a hint that the play is the poet's rendering of the ancient creation myth of the struggle of order and beauty to rise out of primordial chaos, and that in the human world the rejection of the intuitive or feminine function of intelligence by the masculine material mentality leads to destruction.

Viewed in the light of this cosmic profundity, the play becomes Shakespeare's parable of human ignorance, delay and suffering incurred in the outworking of the destiny ordained for mankind.

Matters come to the sharpest crisis of Trojan policy in the second scene of Act II during a council meeting of the Trojan high command, consisting of King Priam and his four sons. The occasion is the receipt of terms of settlement from the Greeks, consisting solely of the restoring of Helen to her husband —

> All damage else — as honour, loss of time, travail,
>   expense,
> Wounds, friends, and what else dear that is concerned
> In hot digestion of this cormorant war —
> Shall be struck off.
>
> Act II, Sc. ii, lines 3-7

Hector advises compliance, basing his decision on a comparison of the value of Helen with that of a Trojan soldier.

Troilus berates him for thinking to measure the infinite honor of their father, the King, in a manner made paltry by "fears and reasons." When Helenus asks if their father does not employ reasons in conducting his affairs, Troilus delivers a lengthy rejoinder, giving the "reason" for the original mission of Paris in molesting the Greeks as that of vengeance for their keeping prisoner "an old aunt," sister of the Trojan King. For Paris to bring home Helen as an incomparable prize was esteemed a worthwhile theft which no moral compunction should be allowed to cheapen.

It is pure Shakespeare for this scene of masculine power, rationalization and quibbling to be interrupted suddenly by the prophetic outburst of Cassandra. Self-interest at the cost of others is spotlighted in the glare of consequences to come.

> Cry, Trojans, cry! Lend me ten thousand eyes
> And I will fill them with prophetic tears.
> . . . .
> Troy must not be, nor goodly Ilion stand;
> Our firebrand brother, Paris, burns us all.
> . . . .
> Cry, cry! Troy burns or else let Helen go.
> > Act II, Sc. ii, lines 102-112

The crisis of our civilization is in that cry. Fire is here the inevitable symbol of uncontrolled passion inflamed by possessiveness and pride. Nor should we overlook the tragedy a civilization brings upon itself by exploiting or failing to recognize not only the dignity of woman, but the feminine principle in life itself.

In the perspective of our twentieth century power conflict and its threat of unparalleled catastrophe, one may scarcely exaggerate the range or force of the meaning Shakespeare brings to focus in Cassandra's warning. The human import is heightened also by the incredulity of the Trojan leaders. Admittedly Cassandra appears to be raving. However, the fact that she is a woman discredits her further, as is also the case with Hector's wife, Andromache, when she later attempts to dissuade her husband from battle by communicating her prophetic dream of his death.

Nothing could be clearer than the poet's realistic intent

to drive home not only the fact but the catastrophic force inherent in man's unperceived self-division and the disaster to which it leads. Extend the meaning of this tragedy, uppointed by Cassandra, to modern man's ignoring of Einstein's warning against a continuance of violence after the splitting of the atom, and the fateful relevance of Shakespeare to the crisis of our time becomes inescapable. The crucial factor in both cases is the closing of one's mind to everything but the arrogance of power. Whether it is man's war against his natural environment or against his fellows, the causative factor is the same. Our culture fails to awaken a Promethean awareness of, and responsibility to, the godlike potentials of the whole man, the heart of Shakespeare's cosmic-human vision.

It is not exaggerating the issue to point out that in all of the plays there is no equivalent example of the force with which the poet brings home the need and power of intuition to reveal the consequences of masculine onesidedness in the pursuit of mind-created ends. Shakespeare's central intent in this play is not to satirize Greek heroes, as critics have held, but to underscore the path of cause and effect by which man's internal self-division between head and heart leads to war.

In the present instance it is not the Greeks but the Trojans who are being satirized. Following Cassandra's outburst, the cutting edge of the immediate response by Priam's sons takes a sudden ironic turn when Hector, after an eloquent appeal to "moral philosophy" and to "Nature" in support of justice and therefore of Cassandra, blandly reverses himself in favor of Troilus' argument for keeping Helen as an incentive to valor, honor, renown and glory. From here on the doom of Troy is sealed, and the death of Hector at the hands of Achilles' Myrmidons — a final touch of humiliation and satire on both sides — is sealed.

It remains to point up some of the facts and implications of the inner story of Troilus who, in his relation to Cressida, reveals himself still more intimately as a type of modern self-divided man. The relation of his emotional malaise to his war psychosis goes far to typify and explain the hazard of our time. In a further sense it reveals the resourcefulness of art in bringing to light the hidden processes at work beneath the dichotomies of thinking which now so crucially divide life in the United States.

Broadly speaking, the unfinished task of Troilus is most intimately human. It is to find out what he is in the midst of the forces playing deceptively around him and through him. His tragedy is his failure, first in war and then under the testing of true and false love, to discover the truth of his own being. Failing this, he is unable to reach the point at which his self-responsibility and his social responsibility coincide.

The United States was founded as a new venture toward solving this problem of the ages: that of bridging the seemingly unbridgeable chasm of dualism in the individual man and in society. All of Shakespeare can be said to revolve on this same issue.

The final truth of the plays is that each man is ultimately his own bridge, the very axis of an understanding that is required to be specific and comprehensive at the same time. Thus we arrive once more at "the poles of truth" on which the plays turn, with every character seen as gravitating toward or away from this pivotal unity in himself according to his self-determination. In the character of Troilus we come to Shakespeare's most poignantly intimate case study of the emotional aspects of this struggle. The interweaving of the private Troilus-Cressida love story with the inter-realm scandal of Paris and Helen and the war issue springing from it increases the range and deepens the subtlety and import of the entire play.

It is by no accident that the intimate discussion between Troilus and Cressida on the subject of love and truth occurs in the exact middle of the play. At this point truth and cunning, love and conscience openly confront each other, with Pandarus typically serving as the self-acknowledged "broker" between them! Words of extraordinary implication come from the lips of Cressida when she artfully taunts Troilus:

> . . . but you are wise;
> Or else you love not; for to be wise and love
> Exceeds man's might; that dwells with gods above.

In reply Troilus speaks with mixed yearning and doubt:

> O that I thought it could be in a woman, —
> As, if it can, I will presume in you, —
>
> Act III, Sc. iii, lines 162-166

From this point on, the seeming balance of forces in the issue takes a downward turn for the Trojans, beginning with the amorous intentions of Troilus and ending with the predicted fall of Troy. Psychologically the original motivation of Paris is reflected in that of Troilus, with military conflict, closely associated with lust, as a form of violence, resulting in a total Trojan defeat. This is the meaning of Cassandra's reference to "Our firebrand brother, Paris" and her prediction, "Troy burns."

The real victim Shakespeare is depicting in the play is love. This is why the play is so intensely modern as a study of blind force induced by passion and why it reflects so strikingly the crisis of our time. In point of loyalty to religious principles, we may sense more than incidental significance in the fact that Cressida, a Trojan, is willingly exchanged by her father, Calchas, a priest, for Antenor, a valued Trojan prisoner of the Greeks. The meaning of this is evident when we consider Calchas' statement that he had "abandoned Troy" because of his devotion to the service of Jove.

This episode provides a transition to what follows as the true test of love between Troilus and Cressida. Her shallow, coquettish nature appears when she encourages the advances of the Greek commander Diomedes, and we see the full import of the role played by Pandarus, Cressida's uncle, and the sullen Greek, Thersites, in their cynical comments on the lecherous way of life.

These problems reach a climax in the second scene of Act V, matching in their personal intensity the fateful challenge of public policy decision which Cassandra had prophesied. In both instances the crisis is sharpened by being focused in the mind of Troilus. It is in him that Shakespeare points up the close relation existing between war, lust and violence in the elementary nature of man.

The scene opens with a visit of Diomedes to Cressida at her father's tent. The encounter turns out to be a miniature theater in itself, with Troilus and Ulysses as spectators.

Diomedes has come to claim a love token Cressida had sworn to give him, but which she now artfully plays at refusing. He prepares to leave, but she calls him back and begins her further game by stroking his cheek, a sight hard for Troilus to endure. When Diomedes asks for at least "some" token, she goes to her room and returns, handing him a military sleeve, the very keepsake which Troilus had given her.

What follows strains Troilus' openly avowed capacity for at least "outward" patience. During a verbal give-and-take between Cressida and Diomedes, she hands him the sleeve but immediately demands its return. He asks four times to know whose sleeve it is, and is as often refused. Cressida finally allows Diomedes to take the sleeve, though still refusing to give the owner's name, and immediately after having asked him not to visit her again, she pleads with him not to leave. At this vacillation Diomedes shows his dislike of "fooling," and expresses his intention not to return. However, he completely reverses himself and agrees to remain.

When after a brief interval Diomedes leaves, Cressida bids farewell to the absent Troilus in a monologue, acknowledging that she now looks on him with but one eye while with the other she is gazing with her heart at Diomedes.

During the scene just enacted Cressida has openly accused herself of falseness, yet in the course of her swiftly fluctuating impulses she has thought to dispose of the crisis by assuming it is past. At the next moment, however, she is obliged to face her duplicity. Confessing that her state of dividedness is a failing common to her sex, she closes with the generalization that "Minds swayed by eyes are full of turpitude." (Act V, Sc. ii, line 112)

Her honest admission of weakness ends Cressida's part in the play.

This passage is unsurpassed as a brief, incisive portrayal of woman at a stage of growth governed by passionate instability. As intimate drama it also serves as a contrast to the image of woman presented by Shakespeare's heroines already discussed. By this means the poet has provided for laying bare the still subtler crisis of self-knowledge in Troilus whose agonizing ordeal is the central problem of the play and has a bearing on our modern world.

Ulysses is ready to leave, since for him the episode is conclusive. But for Troilus the moment has arrived when his inmost nature demands a clarification of the experience he has just endured. He insists on lingering in order

> . . . to make a recordation to my soul
> Of every syllable that here was spoke.
> Act V, Sc. ii, lines 116-117

It is significant to recall here that when Cassandra uttered her prophetic warning about the fate of Troy unless Helen were restored to Menelaus, the meaning of the issue had failed to penetrate Troilus' obdurate passion for Trojan "honor" and victory by force. Now, however, the shell of his pride of status which he had rationalized as patriotism was broken and he was obliged to face the immediate challenge of truth to self-understanding.

What, then, was the real meaning of what he had just witnessed? Its substance was so contrary to what he had known, and the reversal of Cressida's infatuation had been so sudden that he could not delay in coming to terms with his own mind in an effort to keep his sanity. As he told Ulysses, in effect, the elements of faith and hope remaining in his heart were so strong that he could not believe his senses and was ready to doubt if Cressida had actually been present.

It is important to recognize Shakespeare's wisdom in arranging the presence of Ulysses as a fatherly witness and mentor at this moment of crisis for Troilus. His manner is quietly firm and reasoned in dealing with the impassioned youth.

The climax comes after Troilus pins his disbelief in Cressida's presence first on a general appeal to faith in womanhood, then on the theory that there are seemingly two Cressidas, one his and one "Diomed's." This notion he immediately discredits in an appeal to the law of "unity itself."

Caught finally on the horns of his dilemma, he declaims

against the "madness of discourse" which sets up its own contradiction in the form of "bifold authority." Having reached this point, he turns finally upon the irrationality in himself in words which are Shakespeare's most telling single summation of man's interior conflict.

> Within my soul there doth conduce a fight
> Of this strange nature, that a thing inseparate
> Divides more wider than the sky and earth;
> And yet the spacious breadth of this division
> Admits no orifex for a point as subtle
> As Ariachne's broken woof to enter.
>
> Act V, Sc. ii, lines 145-150

In thus sharply pinpointing the issue of self-dividedness and warfare in the individual man, the poet has epitomized the cause of the Graeco-Trojan war and of all war. It is his key statement of our human error, inevitable at a certain stage of growth, in narrowing down the universality of life itself, the life we *are,* into the fragmented and conflicting aspects our minds seize upon in their exclusively separated, hence opposing, identifications of our true selfhood.

In the intense inner drama of Troilus' emotional and mental conflict we witness the working of a psychic vortex of such compulsive severity that it could stand as a universal type image of man's agony of partitioned being. The seeming hopelessness of his condition is sealed, furthermore, by his own conviction that there is no opening left in his consciousness for entry of the least ray of help in the form of "Ariachne's thread," actually the spider-thread of intuition, capable of releasing him from self-entrapment in his divided mind.

In other words, Troilus' unconscious rejection of the symbolic meaning and liberating truth hidden in the myth serves us as a stark example of the tragedy of modern man's habitual refusal to look past the seeming finalities of his physical, emotional, and mental conditioning to an intuitively perceivable mystery of reality, unity, and freedom which is present at all times in life and in himself. When, as today and under the influence of fear, this same obsessive refusal occurs on an international scale, we have a world drifting toward a vortex of incalculable destructiveness.

The fatal mistake of Troilus, both as a Trojan leader and in his private life, was his conclusion that there was no room anywhere between heaven and earth for release from his own self-imprisonment in a world of rivalry and force. In the play, as Shakespeare intended, we are witnessing two phases of the same human error the world over: the false absolutism of the material mind. The reference to Ariachne is expressly Shakespeare's and refers by implication to the voice of Cassandra, whose warning Troilus and his brothers had failed to heed, thus bringing on the doom of Troy.

In the next scene a final opportunity is given to Priam, Cassandra, and Hector's wife to avert this fate by persuading Hector not to fight. Sensing the fact that Troy's fate hangs on Hector's decision, they act with eloquent urgency to combine their warnings, but to no avail. Hector's wife, like Caesar's, cites dreams of "shapes and forms of slaughter," yet Hector brushes them off as irrelevant and is offended when she urges Priam not to yield decision to him. As she leaves, at Hector's command, Troilus pours ridicule on these feminine "bodements" as nothing but the speech of a "foolish, dreaming, superstitious girl."

So much then for the vaunted sufficiency of the separated masculine half of human intelligence. The self-dividedness in Troilus, presented as an intimate type case, prevails also in Hector under the guise of duty to the city or state, rather than to justice, and Hector dies ignominiously at the hands of Achilles' craftily assembled Myrmidons.

This brings to focus the far-reaching implications of Ulysses' matchless speech found in the third scene of Act I, beginning with line 75. In his statement of the law of correspondences we have a partial unfolding of the unbroken chain of order and proportion to which Bacon alluded in his *Novum Organum*: The likenesses "between the architectures and fabrics of things natural and things civil" are not to be regarded as "only similitudes and fancies," but rather as "the same footsteps of nature treading or printing upon different subjects." Thus Shakespeare accords with the Baconian philosophy of science in emphasizing the law of identity in differences, of oneness in diversity, of "union in partition." This perspective links man inseparably with the universe of which he is a miniature replica and is to become a fully conscious citizen. Such a meaning is far removed from the interpretation some commentators have given Ulysses' speech as *merely* a glorification of Tory politics!

The aim of Ulysses is to suggest a linkage between the law-governed order of the heavens as centered in the sun and the patterning of human communities, including schools, brotherhoods, commerce, and family relations. While war is going on, but at a moment of debate, he is conveying the over-all principle of man's sublimest natural image of harmony.

In this speech Shakespeare drives home the point that the universe is the image of an infinite Intelligence in the process of reproducing itself in man. The corollary follows that man cannot cease from violence and achieve a harmonious order in himself until he awakens his own self-knowledge of this truth and begins to live it. Otherwise this healing sunlike beneficence is perverted into a wolf-like destructiveness, overturning the rule of balance and justice.

Ulysses speaks as the true sage in his analysis of the weakness of the Greek chain of command — a chaos created by the mockery and insubordination of Achilles, which has infected other leaders among the Greeks, and undermined Agamemnon's authority and leadership. He concludes:

> And 'tis this fever that keeps Troy on foot,
> Not her own sinews. To end a tale of length,
> Troy in our weakness (stands) not in her strength.
> Act I, Sc. iii, lines 135-137

Ulysses' treatment of the "fever" he detects proves him wily as well as wise in dealing with the foibles of human nature. He is the master mind and author of the scheme which eventually brings Achilles out of his subversive idleness, and restores power and order to Agamemnon's leadership. The inference is clear, that in a personality or in an army, the factions must yield to the greater purpose. This done, the story of the war, with the parallel tragedy of Troilus and of Troy, gathers momentum for its inevitable conclusion.

The American Scene

We come now to the question posed in the title of this chapter. We are in a position to gather up the psychic and philosophical import of all of the plays we have considered and to focus this in a symbolic manner on the present American scene as sharply as the implications of *Troilus and Cressida* warrant.

The United States stands once again, as in the Civil War, at the crossroads in a crisis of self-division. It has become involved in a national contradiction of aims and values which threaten the disunion of that which is united. Specializations of knowledge motivated by profit have far outdistanced the reconciliation of human justice with the total being of man. Indeed the very idea of the totality of being, both in oneself and in the world, has been distorted and rendered suspect by being confused with totalitarianism. The whole problem was summed up by the late professor of philosophy at Harvard, Ralph Barton Perry, as that of "how to be total without being totalitarian." Our remaining discussion of Shakespeare will bear directly on this issue as it refers both to man and to the nation.

The many implications of wisdom in Ulysses' speech point in a striking manner to the scheme of distributive justice in the government of the United States. In large measure these implications anticipate the Newtonian science of cosmic equilibrium, the solar laws of checks and balances from which the over-all concept of the new American system was chiefly derived. In combination with the best tradition of the Hanoverian kings, these three factors together formed a strong historical bridge between England and the American experiment.

It was inevitable that the spectacle of cosmic harmony afforded by the simultaneous revolution of planets on their own axes and around the sun should become an accepted image of democratic freedom and order, when provided with a balance of legislative, judicial, and executive functions.

This emphasis on an identity of laws is what Bacon meant by the sameness of the footsteps of nature imprinted on different subjects. In the present case our reference is to cos-

mic and human governments. It is the force of this identity
which gives meaning to Ulysses' words and substantiates the
truth in the misunderstood relationship between the terms
"liberty" and "equal" in the Declaration of Independence.

Unfortunately the problem of equality or justice has been
the unsolved issue since the founding of the nation. It is
obvious that individual differences in appearance, capacity, and character are enormous, offering as much variety as
do features of the landscape. Thus by natural right, not
merely human concession and sufferance, every man is equally free with every other to think, believe, grow, and perfect
himself. Seen in this light, the assumed license to deprive
one's fellows of opportunity for the constructive use of their
qualities is a violation of life's impartiality and entails mutual tragedy.

These observations are in accord with the Shakespearean
perspective of the laws of harmony between man and nature.
The living force which flows through the plays is revealed
as the wisdom of nature, while the poetry, symbolism, and
dramatic designing are the modes by which this wisdom is
conveyed to human consciousness, to be absorbed in varying
degrees as inspiration and expressed in enlightened action.

Much of what has thus far been implicit in our discussion
now begins to be explicit as applied to man's political and
social experiment in the western hemisphere. In this sense
Shakespeare's vision of man constitutes a guiding yet only
partially comprehended source of light in the unfolding of
the American dream.

It now remains to explore more fully the parallels between
the personal ordeal of self-dividedness in Troilus and the
crisis existing collectively in the United States.

This second area of separative thinking stems from a
legacy of scientific thought to the effect that the universe,
after being divinely created, was left to run itself like a
clock. Western man has continued to follow this materialistic assumption of an extra-cosmic deity, a God considered
as apart from the universe and not *as* the universe. This
has led to his disregard of the omnipresence of life and consciousness in nature as well as in himself.

It was inevitable that this theory of division in the universe, analogous to the dividedness in Troilus, should result in the wholesale violation of the balance of nature occurring with the advances of modern science.

Our transition from the tragedy of the past in *Troilus and Cressida* to that which is now being enacted in the United States is but a step. The human issue in both cases is the meaning of life and the will to its realization, for man has not only the incentive but also the capacity for individual self-transformation. However, being caught up in material preoccupations which lead to social injustices and political hatreds, he has ignored his divine possibilities as unrealistic.

How, then, can man in the United States, a nation racially and socially divided down the middle and lacking a present culture to integrate it, succeed in finding in himself his needed center of undividedness? The image of the United States is now that of a modern Troilus busily engaged in amassing thermonuclear weapons and radioactive poisons. Behind all this is a chasm of self-division, wider than the distance between sky and earth. This image exists for other nations also in varying degrees.

Trojan pleading for the House of Priam and its glory in war has been replaced further by its equivalent in governmental rhetoric, ambiguity, and self-contradiction. The chief difference is the modern advance in the organization and communication of sophisticated self-deception. It can be said of the typical citizen of most countries that he looks everywhere but in himself for the depth of understanding he requires for the solution of his problems. His increasingly desperate need is for a positive inner revolution by which alone he may transcend his competitive mentality of force and the destruction to which it leads. It is likewise unfortunate that instead of the services of Ulyssean philosophers as guides to government, political technicians are employed.

We now pass to the symbolic implications of Ulysses' reference to the sun. For him the sun is not only the center of our immediate cosmic system, the source of its energy and its throne of natural authority. It is the "med'cinable" or healing "eye" of all that exists within the range of its influence. It is the universal symbol of the perfection of inner being which man is destined to discover as a principle within himself.

The Reverse Seal of the United States of America, printed though it is on every one dollar bill, is recognized, studied and revered by almost no one as the symbol of an intended destiny of the nation. This Seal has no parallel in modern history. The motto, *Novus Ordo Seclorum,* signifying "A New Order of the Ages," indicates the newness of the great American experiment in free and orderly relations, a sense of which was immortalized anew by Lincoln in his address at Gettysburg.

Corresponding to Shakespeare's "med'cinable eye," the sunlike source of radiance at the center of the triangle hangs in space to denote the infinitude of the essential self in man. The meaning is identical with that of the Christ saying, "If thine eye be single, thy whole body shall be full of light." This symbol similarly illumines Shakespeare's dramatic picturing of man's ascent to superhuman vision, where he takes upon himself "the mystery of things," as did Lear, Hamlet and, in still greater measure, Prospero.

Overlooking the Raritan River on the outskirts of New Brunswick, New Jersey, is a mansion dating back to the pre-Revolutionary War days. On the railing of a flight of stairs of the main hall are cuts and gashes allegedly left by the sabers of Hessian soldiers. Of chief note, however, is the gilded image of a bird mounted above a doorway at the far end of the hall. At first glance one might take the bird for an eagle, but the body is slimmer, the wings are shorter and the head is relatively small. A closer inspection reveals the conventional figure of a phoenix, ancient symbol of regeneration.

In the many stories told about the history of the Seal of the United States there is one statement made that is of great interest in this connection. Manly Hall, in a short book entitled *The Secret Destiny of America**, devoted a chapter to the meaning of the emblems on the Seal. He refers to the fact that among the designs originally submitted as the appropriate emblem, several showing the phoenix on its nest of flames were submitted.

---

* Philosophical Research Society, Los Angeles, 1944.

The phoenix was the fabulous bird in ancient Egyptian mythology that lived 500 years, then consumed itself in fire, rising again to live another long life. It was the symbol of regeneration — of the "twice-born" who were the possessors of divine wisdom — and refers therefore to initiation into the ancient mysteries.

The question arises: was it the original hope of some of the founding fathers that this symbol of human aspiration to the highest good should be the central motif on the Great Seal?

As a symbol the pyramid reaches back to early Egyptian sources and forward to a timeless future. The combination of the pyramid and all-seeing eye with the phoenix seems more fitting than with the eagle, a military symbol from the days of the Roman Empire. The bird holds in its beak the motto *E Pluribus Unum,* meaning "The One Composed of the Many." This is the cosmic law of unity-in-diversity applied to the principle of human federation.

To the founding fathers the discovery of America was related to dimensions of depth in man's discovery of himself. Thoreau's admonition in the last chapter of *Walden* is pertinent: "Be a Columbus to whole new continents and worlds within you, opening new channels not of trade but of thought."

Applied to the American experiment, the Seal throws rays of light far into the future. At the same time it implies a constant challenge here and now in the direction of a cultural goal to be reached by men who may be healed, made whole and new by a rediscovery of America within themselves. Thus the Seal symbolizes both a new man and a new continent of thought. It was to help unfold this new type of consciousness that the American experiment in freedom and equality was set in motion. Similarly the aim of our adventures in Shakespeare has been to point up the universality of these principles as they pertain to just such an enlightened collective effort toward a freer, happier world.

The modern implication widens greatly when we add two statements from modern scientists. In his *Physics and the Modern World* Eddington called upon his fellow scientists to "place consciousness in the fundamental position." Like-

wise Schroedinger, who helped formulate the quantum theory, ventured in his little book *What is Life?* to share his
conviction that "Consciousness is a singular of which the
plural is unknown." In these ways the unitary principle
underlying all of Shakespeare, the Bible and the Reverse
Seal of the United States receives confirmation.

It is appropriate to note that many efforts of a broadly
cultural, religious, humanitarian and patriotic character
have marked the history of the nation since its beginning
with a view to implementing various integrative resources
of knowledge. The list of societies or foundations created for
the purpose is a long one, but a few examples may be mentioned for the range of their cultural purposes and approach.

One, The Theosophical Society, founded in New York in
1875, undertook as its mission a working synthesis of the
world's religions, sciences, arts, and philosophies with a
view to promoting a universal brotherhood of mankind.
After World War II the United Nations was established
as an international forum and quasi-judicial, moral, and
political authority for voicing and implementing world
thought toward peace. In educational circles, the Center for
the Study for Democratic Institutions, formed in recent
years at Santa Barbara, California, with a staff of brilliant
Fellows, consultants, journalists, and educators drawn from
many parts of the country, has pioneered in focusing human
intelligence intensively yet broadly on the problems of the
nation.

As we evaluate these various efforts in the light of Shakespeare, some suggestive conclusions may appear from correspondences perceived in three different areas: first, the
laws which hold the plays together as they revolve on their
poles of truth; second, those which relate atom and sun to
man; third, those which unite the fifty states of the American Commonwealth in a single federation. Thus our understanding may be stretched to comprehend the parallelism
of these different realms.

The words of Thoreau are enlightening. "Your scheme
must be the framework of the universe: all other schemes
will soon be ruins." The problem is the ageless one in new
form: man's awakening to his Promethean responsibility

for attaining self-unitedness by transcending his self-division. Failure in this was the tragedy of Troilus, and success in it is the issue now confronting man in the United States.

A Shakespearean dimension of meaning for our time may be found in the frontier experience of 19th century American pioneers in crossing the Great Divide en route to the far West. The hazards and hardships of the journey were extreme, yet one of the numerous books on the great West pictured a vista cut through the mountains, with farther scenes of travel to the coastal plain. To the early settlers this was a vision of opportunity to be obtained by surmounting physical or geographical division. Yet such an intimate engagement with the landscape undoubtedly awakened overtones of life potentials and values belonging to man's inner world as well.

The Shakespearean view of life may thus be brought to bear figuratively on the New World experiment, the latter consisting of an inward journey over or through the Great Divide in man. Failure to clear the pass is the result of a materially conditioned attitude, a lack of vision, the work of mind imprisoned by an exclusive preoccupation with mechanism at the cost of ideas in depth.

It is across such a divide that man must pass before he is capable of taking upon himself "the mystery of things" and entering the Shakespearean world of his own eventual kingship.

A visit to the Grand Canyon can be a symbolic experience of this kind. The great scene winds away like a colossal mirror of destiny in which eternity seems to be gazing at itself, while the visitor can gain only momentary intimations, if at all, that the majestically receding forms he sees reflect aspects of his own yet undiscovered being.

Nevertheless if he learns to be similarly silent, patient, and open, he may become his own pioneer in newly discovering America and himself. He may become aware of the truth that all experiences, light or dark, happy or tragic, have a meaning identical with that of the Canyon or of Shakespeare's plays stretching before him and behind him with the wonder of a heretofore unimagined beauty and significance. Whitman suggested that artists and poets should pay "feeding visits" to the great spectacle of the Grand Canyon.

Perhaps it may be suggested that in these analogies we have keys to the purpose and meaning of the "new order of the ages," symbolized by the Reverse Seal. "The more's the pity," as Bottom would say, that education is oriented so completely away from these mysteries of man and from an awareness of the principle in consciousness which makes the understanding possible.

The English novelist, J. B. Priestley, wrote with great beauty of the Grand Canyon in a book entitled *Midnight on The Desert.** No description of the Grand Canyon seems comparable in imaginative range of grasp and illumination. The following sentence indicates his understanding of how an American might well feel as he gazes into its majesty: "If I were an American I should make my remembrance of it the final test of men, art and policies." He concludes with this statement: "Every member or officer of the Federal Government ought to remind himself, with triumphant pride, that he is on the staff of the Grand Canyon."

Across the entire continental width and topographical grandeur of the United States there is, as in Shakespeare, a natural flow of life, a sweep of imagery alive with influences of beauty, inspiration, and power. If thoroughly absorbed, these may go far toward enabling man to experience a relation to things and to his fellows as they really are. This cosmic ecological rhythm has its own momentum and can rise to knowledge of itself in mankind when the silence of its immanence is not violated. Today the shadow of a colossal tragedy falls across the world, owing to the dictatorship of man's mind in producing technological nightmares of exploitation, pollution, warfare, speed, and death. As a result man is out of focus with himself and the nation is self-divided.

In this Troilus-like situation it is necessary to unite two different sets of facts, just as a horizon line unites while it divides nearness and distance, earth and sky, finitude and infinitude. For Troilus the division in himself seemed hopeless and absolute because he could not find a unitary prin-

* Harper & Brothers, New York, 1937

ciple in his being. In Ulysses, on the contrary, this principle
had awakened to self-awareness because he had ascended a
ladder of consciousness leading unbrokenly from his emotions to his reason, then to his imagination, and then to
intuitive vision. At that point he could speak with wisdom
because he incarnated it. He had reached self-knowledge
where the cosmic order of the world and in himself were
unified and in a sense identical.

Light on this mystery may be found in the following passage from Tagore's luminous book on *Personality.*

> There is a point where in the mystery of existence
> contradictions meet; where movement is not all move-
> ment and stillness is not all stillness; where the idea
> and the form, the within and the without, are united;
> where infinite becomes finite without losing its infinity.
> If this meeting is dissolved, then things become unreal.

It is difficult to find a simpler yet more illuminating
statement of the crisis now faced by the United States in
dealing with its problem of disunitedness. Clearly the particular point at which a solution becomes possible is the vital
centering of intelligence indicated by the All-Seeing Eye
at the middle of the triangle in the Reverse Seal. This is
no mere abstraction. It represents the convergence and
radiation of man's total forces of consciousness, the lines of
his creative energy or "value intensities," to use a Jungian
term.

A passage from Jung's *Modern Man in Search of a Soul**
is pertinent: "In my picture of the world there is a vast
outer realm and an equally vast inner realm; between these
two stands man, facing now one and now the other, and
according to his mood or disposition, taking the one for the
absolute truth by denying or sacrificing the other." These
are indeed the poles of truth on which the plays of Shakespeare turn.

In citing these passages we are defining the need and
nature of the task now confronting America. From the
time of Franklin, Jefferson and Washington the central ideal
of the nation has been the pursuit of happiness, the uniting

---

* Harcourt, Brace, World, Inc., New York.

of earth and heaven in the life of the common man. Without this blending, neither freedom nor order can truly exist. This is what Ulysses is saying, and only a culture which implements this vision can heal the world's sickness of violence and disorder.

Ulysses, interpreted in a Baconian light and placed in confrontation with Troilus, sets the stage for a right perception of the wisdom of the Great Seal. The oneness of the union of the States affirmed on the obverse side by the motto *E Pluribus Unum* and illumined on the other by the centering of the motto *Novus Ordo Seclorum,* the New Order of the Age, defines the mission and opportunity of the individual man at a point where idea and form converge and from which they radiate. This blending of particulars with universals is the goal toward which the education of the whole man must be directed, and to this end the meaning of Shakespeare in universalizing all human experience has never been fully understood or applied.

In the Pacific Northwest the mountain named Rainier, but by the Indians called Tahomah, "the mountain that was God," stands as another silent mentor.

The writer had been driving southward along the coastal highway. During the day heavy clouds hung unbrokenly at a three thousand foot level, and by late afternoon all hope of seeing the great mountain had been abandoned. However, a moment arrived when a glance to the left revealed a sunlit view of the majestic form, its upper ten thousand feet towering above the clouds and hanging like a pink and white apparition in the sky.

To feel the silent wonder of that mountain Presence is to experience a principle at the center of one's being, a power of truth and love capable of lending a new height of purpose and meaning to life and to the land one lives in. It helps to know what to do in dealing with one's mind and in dissolving the cloud of fear and dividedness which hangs over the nation.

There it stood in the glory of its massive serenity, majestically poised in the power of its own law, looking down on a nation unmindful of the equivalent of all this in the symbolism of the Great Seal. The secret of the godlike inspiration conveyable by mountain and Seal alike lies in the spirit of reality and infinitude radiating from a point of consciousness which awaits man's discovery in himself and the universe alike.

This glimpse of the mountain was a Shakespearean revelation. There it stood in the healing sunlight of wholeness, image of the Great Seal and symbol of man as he is to become: the conqueror of his illusions by means of the absolute principle of consciousness in him which gives life, wisdom and power. Here was the American dream, the Shakespearean vision, the Promethean prophecy of man as his own future Ulysses and Prospero, poised on the throne of his destiny in the realm of being.

INDEX OF PLAYS AND CHARACTERS CITED